Isabel Crossley

Falconsdale

Falconsdale

Howard Jones

Blackie: Glasgow and London

ISBN 0 216 89660 6

Blackie and Son Limited
Bishopbriggs, Glasgow G64 2NZ
Fitzhardinge Street, London W1H 0DL

Filmset by Thomson Litho, East Kilbride
Printed in Great Britain by Robert MacLehose & Co. Ltd., Glasgow

Contents

The Red King 1

FALCONSDALE. It lies beneath me as I write. I close my eyes, but still I see it, limned on the curtain of my lids with all its detail, in all its myriad colours. There is the blue of high heaven and the white cloud clinging to the peaks, as if some mighty rider of the skies had sped this way and left a shredded cloak behind. There is the deep green of bracken lower down, and lower still the bright green of pastures where many sheep are folded. Under the steep slopes one half of the valley is washed with shadow, a shadow so deep that it is almost black. The other half is a dazzle of white in the morning sun. And you can see there the silver ribbon of Ravensmere and Heronwater curling into the distance, and the narrow strip of land, like a giant's thumb, which holds the lakes apart.

On this day of high summer nothing stirs except the grasses and the heather all about you. There is no sound except the moan of the western wind as it sweeps across the fells. And you have the feeling that this valley is eternal, that nothing ever changes here. Just as you see it now, on this second anniversary of the death of William Rufus, so it was when the Romans camped near by a thousand years ago, so it will be a thousand years from now.

On such a day as this, and almost in this very spot, my story has its start. I was a small, fair-haired, fair-skinned boy, and I had climbed here to work on a Latin exercise Father Benedict had set me. I stretched in the lee of a boulder and closed my eyes and started to recite aloud the exercise which I had laboriously written out the previous evening.

"Barbari se celeriter receperunt . . ."

A soft wind fanned my face, all about me was golden sunlight. My mind wandered to a bow and a dozen arrows which I had hidden in a cavity of the stone wall yonder. Presently I went to the wall and took out the bow, one of a pair old Tom had made for me. The arrows I had made myself, cutting them from birch wood and fletching them with goose feathers.

The trunk of a burnt spruce served me as King of the Barbarians, and I drew off thirty paces and put three arrows into his black old heart, and then three more, all within a space which a man could cover with his hand. I was a marksman even then, thanks to Tom's patient teaching. Long ago, before age and rheumatism had settled in his joints, he had fought in Wales under our own Earl Bueth, whom men call the Falcon; and even amongst the Welsh, who are fine bowmen, there was none to beat Tom for accuracy and speed.

I was still practising with the bow when I spied Tom striding a path high above me, his white hair streaming from his shoulders like a mane. He paused and beckoned. I put my bow away in the hiding place and clambered up to him.

"He's a-come, Alan," said he. "The devil's a-come!"

"You mean Count Ralf?"

Tom spat. "Ralf Meschin's there, no doubting. But I mean a worser devil than him! I mean the Red King, Rufus, who's camping down by Windermere with the biggest army ever man set eyes on—so they say, so they say! Come and see, Alan."

He set off with his limping, long-legged stride, and I tagged on at his heels. For all that he was cruelly crippled in one hip, he could move as nimbly as a goat over the slopes, for he was a man of the fells, and it was all I could do to keep pace with him.

For a long while he did not speak, and I thought he must have forgotten me. But at last he paused, and with his gentle, radiant smile that sent a warmth right through me (for I looked on Tom as my one loving friend) he asked if he pressed the pace too fast. And when I answered no, he pointed upwards, and said:

"From yon shoulder, we shall see—what we shall see! Come ye, Alan."

We climbed to a hummock of lichen-coated rock poised on the lip of a precipice like a drowsing beast, and from there we looked down as an eagle looks from its eyrie. We saw the yellow thread of a road driving northwards to Carlisle, and the roofs of the town the Romans built and called Galava. We saw the waters of Windermere shimmering like a burnished shield, and on the flat lands edging the northern shore of the lake we saw the camp of England's king.

There was row upon row of tents, tents big and small, brown and white, so many that you could not count them, and set so close that the lines merged in the distance. It was a great sprawling city of tents, with here and there green open spaces, and pennons fluttering like coloured sparks in the wind, and smoke rising in a thin brown mist from the kitchens.

You could sense the secret life that pulsed down there in that great tented city. If you fixed your gaze on one of the green spaces, you would see an ambling speck that could have been a man, or a tiny, dark flickering shape that could have been a trotting horse. They passed and re-passed, some quickly, some with infinite slowness, and the brown smoke-plumes rose, and the pennons fluttered; and because the wind was blowing from the peaks into the dale, you could hear nothing, a solid silence overhung it all. I think it was the silence of that monstrous camp which so frightened me.

"A great army, truly," Tom said after a long while. "The greatest army ever I seen."

I asked: "What do they want, Tom?"

"What does any army want but to make a war?"

"Will they make war on us?"

"Perhaps, Alan. He hates us, that rogue of a Rufus. But they are saying he means to march on Carlisle, and drive out Dolfin and the Scots, and build there a castle to put chains on the north as his father, the Bastard, first put chains on the south."

"If they fight with us, we will kill them all," I said. But looking down on those countless tents, I could not in my heart believe it.

Tom was quiet for a minute. Then he gave me a sideways look, and grunted: "We may not fight."

"If they attack us, we will fight," I said. "The Falcon has always fought."

"Don't know, boy," Tom answered slowly. "I am not of Earl Bueth's Great Council."

"We have always fought and won, Tom," I said.

"Nay, Alan, we've not always won. But we've never lost and

that's why these Normans hates us so bitterly. We are a little piece of England that didn't die with Harold Godwinson at Senlac. We defied the Bastard, we defy Ralf Meschin, our feudal overlord, we defy Rufus. Leastaways, that's how I thought till yesternight, when I hears this talk."

"What talk is it?"

"Why, talk that says the Falcon thinks the King of England's strength is overmuch for us."

I thought of Earl Bueth, the Falcon, that gaunt old man whom I found it hard to love, but who was yet, I knew, a brave and fearless leader of his Lakeland people. And I cried out with passion:

"No, Tom, no! He won't betray us!"

"Betray," Tom said slowly, as if he were tasting the word. And again he spat. "Don't know, Alan. It's only talk as I hears, but there's a sameness about the talk that I don't like. They say messengers are going to Rufus tomorrow to see what terms he'll grant us."

I was silent for a while. Then I asked: "What messengers?"

Tom looked away, and answered gruffly: "Benedict, as I hears. And Jarvad the armourer, and Nils, your father, and Edward, your brother. That's as I hears."

"It isn't true!" I cried.

"Yon's a mighty army," Tom said. "It could be true, Alan."

We stayed there a long time, looking down. The sun was dipping beyond Scarigg Crags as we turned back to the Valley.

Father Benedict 2

LONG AGO my father had decided that I should eventually be received into a monastery; and because of this I did not live with him and my brother deep in the dale, but lodged in the small thatched house of Father Benedict on the western shore of Ravensmere.

As I descended the slope, after bidding Tom good night, I could see a rushlight like a distant star in the window. Not till then did I remember my Latin exercise, for my head was crammed with other things, and I braced myself for the punishment to come. But directly I entered the hut I could see that Father Benedict, too, had forgotten the task he had set me.

Without a word he motioned me to the table, ladled out a dish of stew from the pot over the fire, and put it before me. Then he went to the door, and stared out over the lake, smooth as marble in the soft evening light. I gabbled my grace, watching his short, brown-habited figure through the steam rising off my plate.

He was a strange, young old man, small and neat, with dark, sad eyes, a lined face, and hands as smooth as a young girl's. It was a mystery to me then, and it is a mystery to me still, that so much knowledge could be packed into one small tonsured head. He taught me to read and write in English. He taught me mathematics and Latin and French; he taught me about far-off lands and distant seas; and of the stars in heaven, and how their message could be read; and of the glories of God's Kingdom beyond the stars, where dwelt my particular guardian angel, Gabriel, to whom I must regularly pray. He taught me to brew valuable medicines from the herbs in the field, and to heal wounds, and to physic a sick goat.

All these things he taught me, and could have taught me much more, only that my poor head was already stuffed too full for my eleven years.

Benedict in fact was neither monk nor priest. But he had spent three years in a monastery, he always wore the monkish garb, and he was of such a Godly caste of mind that we common people always called him Father Benedict. For my part I went in great awe of him, he was so clever and gifted. He was a man almost without passion; only once did I see him out of temper. He was strict with me, but just and kind. Often I wondered to myself what he would say if he knew of the secret defiance of him and his plans for me that lay deep within my heart.

A year previously he had taken me to the great Abbey at Penrith, where I answered many searching questions put to me by the white-haired Prior. The old man expressed his satisfaction with me, and said that I must return in due time and he would receive me as a novice. But as I stared at his pinched yellow face and sunken jaws there arose in me such a horror of his cloistered way of life that I resolved then and there that I would never, never become a monk. But I never told the Prior or Benedict of this, for I had not so much courage.

I had all but finished my stew when Father Benedict turned back into the room and threw another log on to the fire. I knew I should wait for him to address me first, but I could bear the silence no longer, and I burst out:

"Father, King Rufus is camped by Windermere!"

"I know, my son," said he.

"He has a great army there."

"I know, my son."

"And they say—Father, they say . . ."

"What do they say, Alan? And who says it?"

"Tom says that—that Earl Bueth is sending you, and my brother Edward, and my father, and Jarvad to Rufus to surrender. . . ."

"Tom says too much, my son."

"But, Father, are you going to Rufus—are you?"

"I am going, my son, with your father, and your brother, and Jarvad the armourer."

He stood looking down at me with a strange, withdrawn look on his face as if he could not clearly see me. I felt sick.

I did not want to believe him. I jumped up, shouting:

"Don't go, don't go! Don't surrender to Rufus!"

"Be silent, my son."

"They will kill my brother, they will kill you, they will . . ."

"Be silent, my son," he said again. But I could not be silent. I burst into tears, thinking of my brother, Edward. Father Benedict pushed me gently towards the metal crucifix hanging on the inner wall. "Say your *Credo* and your *Pater Noster*, Alan." And when I did so without faltering or snivelling, for this was the discipline he imposed on me, he said simply: "God be with you. You may go to bed, my son."

I went into the next room and lay down on the wooden bed. Through the doorway I heard Father Benedict whispering at his prayers, and I watched the swing of his shadow as he paced to and fro across the room. Presently he stopped, and I lay still, feigning sleep, listening to the churring note of a nightjar and wondering remotely if it would fly away at midnight to suck at our nanny goats.

My mind was alert and I could not sleep.

I thought of many things. I thought of Father Benedict, and old Tom, and of my brother, Edward; and then I stuffed my knuckles into my mouth for fear that I should cry again, and that Father Benedict would hear me. I thought of the King's camp, and of the King himself, a gross, young, fair-headed man from all accounts; and I thought of his terrifying father, William the Bastard.

My brother and Tom had often spoken to me of the Bastard, whom some called the Conqueror because of his many victories. They told me of his great cruelties and his lust for revenge; and how because of that, we owed it to him that we were men of the Lakes. And they told me of the great revolt in England a few years after the Bastard's victory at Senlac, when King Swein of the Danes had brought his fleet into Humber River; and the Bastard rode swiftly north, then west, then north again, with a great avenging army.

My parents at this time were newly wed and living in the city of York. Then came William the Bastard and laid the city waste, and not the city alone, but all the fair, fine countryside for sixty miles northward. Villages he destroyed, and farms and cattle and crops, and all the means of husbandry; so that a hundred thousand English men, women and children died in the famine, which is more by far than all the stars you can count in the heavens of a winter's night; and that for many a long year afterwards, nothing grew but poisonous weeds in those deserted lands.

The displaced fled in terror, driving their cattle before them when they could. Some went north to the border, for many believed (before the Bastard forced Malcolm of Scotland to swear allegiance) that they would find freedom there. Some went south to the Fens, where the Lord Hereward, son of the Lady Godiva, had raised the flag of freedom at Aldreth. And some trailed north by west to where Earl Bueth, from the crags of our Lakeland mountains, cried defiance. My parents and Father Benedict were of this company.

At that time Benedict was not twenty years old. By birth a Frenchman, he had come to England as a page in the service of one of the Bastard's Norman knights. Indeed, he actually fought under the Bastard's pennon at Senlac, and carried a long scar on his left thigh which had been made by an English sword. But the fearful slaughter in the battle sickened him of war and turned his thoughts to God; and a few months later he was received into a monastery not far from the city of York.

Within two years the Bastard marched north for a second time, ravaging with fire and sword. Benedict had not yet taken his final vows, and though he would have been safe within the monastery walls, he felt compelled by pity and brotherly love to join the band of those who fled the Bastard's wrath.

It was a fearful journey. They travelled only by night, lying in hiding during the daylight hours. On a bleak winter's morning, in a spinney on the banks of River Swale, my only brother was born. For the last forty miles, from the dales up across the high fells, Father Benedict carried the new-born baby and my father carried my mother on his back.

You would have thought that William would have been satisfied with all this. But no. Soon he was making a royal progress to Carlisle; and there he installed our feudal overlords, the brothers Ralf and William Meschin, granting them the lands northward from the Bay of Morecambe to the Solway. "The widest and wildest lands of England," said he. "You have but to subdue the rebels and take all the riches that lie therein."

Half a dozen times Count Ralf sent an army into the mountains to subdue the rebels; and half a dozen times they were thrown back. His men and horses were driven into the bogs that lie athwart the old northern road, and there they drowned in hundreds. His rich convoys of food, arms and treasure, moving up the road to Carlisle, were set upon and pillaged, and the attackers vanished like phantoms in the mountain mists. From time to time Count Ralf took prisoners. But never once did he persuade a prisoner to lead him over the secret winding fellside tracks to Falconsdale, where lay the headquarters of his arch enemy, Earl Bueth.

It was a hard living in the mountains, for our soil is thin and the mouths were many. My father, who was tall and strong, laboured in the fields of Heronwater, growing oats and rearing sheep. But he was in heart a fighting man, not a farmer. The fields saw less and less of him; Earl Bueth came to love and to trust him, giving him charge of a squadron of horse and appointing him to his Great Council. My brother Edward, too, was enlisted with my father's squadron though he was little more than a boy.

My poor mother was left alone for long periods, and truly I believe it broke her heart. Fourteen years after they had fled from York across the knobbly backbone of England, I was born; and in giving me life, my mother died.

For that I think my father never forgave me.

He was a good man and a brave man. But we had no love for one another. When I was four years old, Father Benedict, thinking even then that I was quick to learn, suggested that he should have charge of me and train me for a religious life, and my father, without a second thought, agreed. In all the subsequent years he visited me only once at Father Benedict's house by Ravensmere, and it was a meeting that meant nothing to either of us. For we were strangers to each other.

I had no friends of my own age. Apart from Father Benedict, my companions were old Tom and my brother Edward, whom I saw too rarely. But when he could spare the time from his duties, Edward would always come to see me. He was a big, lusty, laughing youth, a wonderful hand with a horse, and with a spear and a short sword. I cannot recall that he ever spoke an unkind or an angry word to me. He was my good companion; he taught me many things, such as riding, swimming, wrestling, and swordplay, and I loved him dearly.

I must have wept silently as I lay in the shadows, watching the play of firelight on the wall of the next room. I felt the wet tears on my cheeks, and I screwed my eyes up tight to staunch them; and I remember hearing again and again the eerie, haunting cry of the nightjar. When next I opened my eyes I saw a broad beam of sunlight slanting through the doorway.

I rose quickly. The next room was empty, nor was there any sign of Father Benedict outside the house. I made a breakfast of milk and rye bread, then went down to the lake and swam in the cold, clear waters. As I swam I saw on the far edge of the lake a flurry of dust raised by a string of horseman. And I knew by secret instinct that there rode Edward and my father and Jarvad and Benedict, on their way to Windermere to seek terms of peace from Rufus, King of England.

I came from the water and stood naked by the reeds, watching them out of sight. Then again I wept with the anguish of my thoughts. As I dressed a swift determination rose in me that I, too, must go to the camp of the English king, to be with Edward and my father. They would arrive a day or two before me, but that did not matter. In any case, I could save a long morning's march by rowing across the lake.

Yes, I must go! I found Father Benedict's rowing boat moored by the landing stage I had helped to build. I rowed across the lake with long and steady strokes.

At the King's Camp

3

I LEFT THE boat amongst reeds on the lake's far shore and set off in my march across the hills. I dropped down into Langwaite Bottom and took a long drink from the ghyll there before climbing to the Pikes, where I rested a while, seeing the Red King's camp far, far off in the misted distance. I descended from the Pikes in the grey of evening and begged some bread from an old woman in a shepherd's hut, saying I had lost my way. That night I rested very comfortably in a birch coppice under Silver Howe. Late on the following afternoon I reached Windermere.

I stood amongst the tents of the great camp, bewildered by everything about me: the bustle, the colour, the smells of men and beasts and cooking meats, the incessant murmur in which were blended men's voices and women's laughter, the beat of hooves, the yelping of dogs, the snapping of pennons in the breeze high over the pavilions. Soldiers in hauberks and woollen tunics passed me, and serving women with dishes and bowls, and once a fine lady trotted by on a horse, her white head veil fastened by a circlet of gold on her forehead.

I stood for some minutes, not knowing which way to turn. All the time I was thinking of Edward, knowing that he was somewhere in this great camp, perhaps very close to me. I must let him know I am here, I thought; I must find him, I must speak with him. But how could I find him without asking, and perhaps betraying myself as a follower of Earl Bueth, a rebel boy from the Valley of the Falcon?

It had astonished me that I had been able to enter the camp without hindrance, without once being questioned. But so it was; nobody seemed in the least interested in me. Presently I started to walk about, with a sort of carelessness in my manner, as if I had a right to be there. I came to some kitchens and the smells brought on an ache of hunger, and I begged something from a cook bent over a fire. He was a young, laughing man, and he called me an impudent young monkey, and gave me a wooden skewer on which were three or four fine hot pieces of meat.

I wandered away and presently fell in with a big, hairy warrior from Flanders, who spoke French with such a gritty accent that at times I could scarcely follow him. He showed me his sword and also his bow, a poor, small thing compared with anything Tom had made. When I asked him if he intended to attack Earl Bueth's rebels in the fells, he spread his big, strong hands.

"I've heard tell of Bueth's men—good bowmen, nimble as goats, they say. But we march where the Red King pleases."

"Shall you march to Carlisle, perhaps, sir?"

"We will that!" said he. "It's been captured from Count Ralf by another damned rebel named Dolfin. But we'll settle accounts with this Seigneur Dolfin, we'll let him see who's master in this land—ach, we will, we will!"

"Have any messengers come from Earl Bueth to parley with the King?" I asked presently, greatly daring.

The man ran his fingers through his thick black hair. "I'll ask King when he invites me to sup at his royal table," he answered, and chuckled deep.

He gave me a swig of sharp-tasting wine from a leather bottle, then turned away. I strolled down the line of tents, and I had scarcely covered fifty paces when there rose, from somewhere on my right, a man's anguished scream.

I stood motionless for a minute, the terrible cry echoing through and through me. I heard shouts, then again the cry—and yet again. I ran towards the cry, I reached an open space. I could see nothing because of the throng of soldiers gathered in front of me; so I wriggled my way through them, fearful of what I might see, but unable to stop myself.

Then I saw.

I saw the King on a stool, a pot-bellied, ruddy-faced man, watching in silence, his left elbow on his knee, his chin supported on the flat of his hand.

I saw Father Benedict standing between two armed men, his eyes averted.

I saw Edward kneeling, his wrists tied to a block. Then the flash of the executioner's sword, the hands flew upwards, I heard the scream. Then Edward slumped on to his face, the executioner turned him with his foot, and again the sword fell and sliced deep into his throat.

I saw the two handless corpses on the grass, and knew them for my own father and Jarvad the armourer.

All this I saw in less time than it takes to count ten. A sort of madness filled me. I ran forward, shrieking, and the executioner turned to face me. Tall and brown and strong was he, and there was blood upon him, upon his face and his bared arms, his sword and his tunic. And Edward, my brother, was at his feet, his life spilling out, darkly staining the bright grass. And the King sat motionless, smiling a little hard smile, supporting his fat chin on his hand. I ran at him, shrieking, and shadows danced about me on the grass, a hand seized me by the hair, a fist sent me crashing down.

I rose, and the coward in me possessed me, and I turned and fled terrified into the ranks of the soldiers gathered around that space. I yelled and beat at them with my fists, and I heard their mocking laughter, and I ran and ran. They did not hinder me, but laughed, and sped me on with slaps and kicks. I ran until I dropped exhausted, my heart hammering wildly in my breast.

When presently I opened my eyes, I saw that the camp of the Red King was far behind me, and that beyond the waters of a beck by which I lay, the Lakeland mountains soared steep and purple into a fair summer sky.

The Manor House 4

FOR MANY days thereafter I lived in a sort of dream, wandering without purpose in strange and distant places. I remember long, shadowed valleys where the air thrummed with the song of tumbling waters, and screes lay thick and treacherous. I remember wide slopes where the wind ran through waist-high bracken in wave upon grey wave; and lakes shimmered like a spread of gems under a white, hot sun. I remember jagged pinnacles from which I beheld the western ocean and, far, far beyond, the mountains of Ireland, like the walls of a distant citadel.

These I remember. But how I lived, or what my thoughts were, in those days, I cannot say. I only know that I was alone always, and that I found it good to be alone. And then, on a bright morning, I came upon a familiar narrow track running in a great arc across the fellside, and I stood there, and all the hurtful memories of Edward came flooding back. I felt an urge to turn and run away, but this I could not do, for somehow I had the belief that the beckoning hand of God had brought me here. So I walked forward down the track, and up through a pinewood which I knew, and when I came into the sunlight on the far side, there was old Tom, standing with his back towards me.

He must have heard my footfall, for he swung about; and his mouth opened wide, and then he came up to me, and dropped his crook, and put his hands on my shoulders.

"Alan," he said. "Alan."

"Yes, Tom."

"Just like you've come from the grave, Alan," he said.

His mouth tightened, and I saw the tears gleam in his fine eyes.

"They killed Edward," I said.

"I know, Alan."

"They killed Edward, and my father, and Jarvad."

"I know, Alan."

"How can you know?"

"I know because of Father Benedict. He saw you in the camp and reckoned they must have killed you, too. But him they durstn't kill, being a man of God. So the Red King sent him back with a gift for Earl Bueth, which he was sworn to deliver safely."

"A gift?" said I. "What manner of gift?"

Tom paused, narrowing his eyes.

"It was the severed right hands of your brother and your father and Jarvad. And the Red King sent word that he'd deal with every rebel and every traitor in that fashion."

"And how did the Falcon answer that?"

"They say he wept."

"Is that all?" I cried bitterly.

"No, Alan, that's not all. There was a Council called and he said that now he would never, never make terms with the Red King. And the Council was with him every man, and each renewed his oath according."

"Edward had to die to make that happen," I said.

Tom was silent for a little. Then said he:

"You're different, Alan."

"How am I different?"

"There's an old look on you that wasn't there before," he said. "Come you down to my hut, you can rest there, and I've food aplenty."

"First I must see Father Benedict," I said. "But I'll be back by sunset."

So I left him and marched on. But presently my grief for Edward welled up anew in me, and the tears streamed down my face as I walked. I felt better for my weeping, though I was thankful Tom was not there to see me. As I descended the slope above Ravensmere, I saw Father Benedict working at his garden. I marched on steadily, and presently stood beside him, waiting for him to speak.

"God's mercy with you, Alan," he said, and put a finger

under my chin, and tilted my face, and looked at me long and searchingly. "You have been crying, my son! Where have you been?"

"I don't know," I said.

"It is three whole weeks since I saw you in the King's camp. What have you been doing since then?"

"I don't know," I said.

"You are troubled, my son. What is it?"

"Father—Father," I said. "There is something I must tell you."

"Tell me, then," he answered, smiling.

"I won't be a monk, Father. I won't go into the monastery."

"You are overwrought, my son," he said. "Come into the house, I'll get some food."

"I won't be a monk!" I shrieked. "I won't go to the monastery! I won't, I won't, I won't!"

He took me by the arm and led me into the house. He made me stand with my eyes on the crucifix on the wall, and for an hour he prayed and talked to me, not in anger but gently and with much firmness. My legs ached, my head throbbed, his voice became a meaningless drone in my ears. Then suddenly I realised that he was waiting for me to speak. I shouted:

"I won't go into the monastery!"

The lines of his face lengthened and deepened. Then again he took my arm and led me out to the lake. We climbed into a boat, and in silence he rowed down the lake to the marshy spit of land at the entrance of Falconsdale. There he tied up, and we walked in silence along the shore of Heronwater, past the kitchens and the bakery and the armourer's shop to the great wooden Manor House by the water's edge.

He bade me stand at the door and disappeared within. After a long while he returned and led me inside. I knew the Manor House well, but I had never been inside before. It was one vast, gloomy hall, with low walls built out from the corners, making, as it were, a number of small private rooms or compartments. In the centre of the floor a log fire burned and the smoke rose in a slender blue spiral to vanish through a squared hole in the roof. There were several doorways unevenly spaced in the walls, leading, I supposed, to other rooms, and in the great hall there were many people, though none took notice of me. Father Benedict guided me past the fire; and there, beyond it, on a low platform against the wall, Earl Bueth sat alone on a great carved seat, with two yellow hounds at his feet. I dropped to my knees, and one of the hounds momentarily lifted his head, looked at me, and went to sleep again.

"Stand," Earl Bueth said.

I stood.

"Look at me."

He was a tiny, frail old man, old beyond my reckoning. His hair was white, his big hooked nose and his moustache were white, the white flesh lay so tight on his cheekbones and his temples that his huge green eyes seemed to stand forth from his head.

"You have been to the Red King's camp, boy?"

"Yes, lord."

"Why did you go?"

"I—I wanted to be with my brother."

"Well, your brother is dead. Your father, too."

"I know. I saw it happen, lord."

"But you came back here! Are you a spy for the son of the Bastard? I have a quick way with spies!"

"Lord, I swear . . ."

"Enough! For years Benedict has laboured to make you ready to serve God. He tells me that you have quick learning, that you write Latin and speak French and calculate with figures. But now you come from the camp of the Bastard's son full of disobedience and refusing to serve God! Is it so?"

"Lord, let me serve you!"

"It was your father's wish that you should be a monk."

"It is the wish of Father Benedict. My father did not care what happened to me."

"But it is a good wish."

"It is a bad wish, lord!"

"Say you so to my face? Why, boy, why?"

"Lord, my heart is here in the fells, not there, imprisoned in a monastery."

The Falcon stirred in his great chair. He pressed his thin hands together, the knuckles cracked. His eyes never left my face, and the chill of them pierced me to the soul. One of the hounds flopped on to its side, its tail twitched.

"I command you," said he, "I command that tomorrow you go to the monastery."

"No, lord," I whispered.

And I hung my head. My heart was pounding, the sight of that pitiless white face was more than I could bear. And truly, I was now so terrified that all my body was in a tremor.

"Look at me!" he said.

I looked at him.

"You disobey me, boy!"

"Yes, lord."

"Do you know that I can have you whipped and branded with irons, and have your eyes gouged out?"

"Yes, lord."

"And you still disobey me?"

"Yes, lord."

"Come close," he said.

I stood before him on the platform, sensing his awful power, fancying that somehow he would kill me on the spot. And then I saw, in the deep depths of those green eyes, a new light—not warmth, for that was scarcely possible, but as it were, a gleam of softness that was almost kindly. He said, without passion:

"What is it you wish then, boy?"

"Oh, let me be a shepherd with old Tom!"

"A shepherd? Will this content you?"

"Yes, yes! But I will serve faithfully as you command me, lord!"

"I shall be better served by a hawk than a sparrow," Earl Bueth said. "Go now and work with Tom, and grow big, and learn obedience—may he not spare a rod across your shoulders! God go with you, Alan."

I knelt and kissed the cold white hand, and walked out joyously into the sunlight.

The Summons 5

FOR THE next four years I lived with Tom in his hut of heather thatch and wattle beneath Birk Crags, and I worked with him, sometimes in the dales where our few kine were herded, sometimes in the woodlands with the swine, but mostly on the fellsides with the sheep. They were happy years for me in many ways, but not entirely so, for reasons which I will explain directly.

I grew up healthy and strong, though I was never big. I loved Tom dearly as I had loved Edward, and I came to feel a sort of love for our wayward, stupid sheep. Tom and I were abroad in all weathers and we were seldom separated. Spring saw us busy with lambing; summer with shearing, and often with crag-bound sheep—animals, that is, who get themselves isolated on some dizzy shelf or pinnacle in search of herbage. Then I would clamber up or down a near vertical wall of rock, or perhaps Tom would lower me on a rope, and I would bring back a couple of bleating lambs, or a terrified old ewe tied to my back, and we would account that a day's work well done.

Winter was no easier, for though we brought the sheep down to the lower slopes, high winds and heavy snow could bring swift disaster. Then you had to go out, no matter how bitter the cold or what the hour of night, and dig your way through the drifts and along the tracks, and you might pass within arm's length of a dozen snowed-in sheep and never know it. For they huddle motionless and silent, and let the falling snow cover them, and there they remain until they starve, or until you find them. And it is wonderful to find them, to bring them to food and warmth, to see the spark of life move again in the glazed, bewildered eyes. You feel like a god, for you have measured your strength against tempest and mountain, and triumphed.

But not all my time was given to sheep or swine or cattle, nor would Tom have had it so. He was as keen as was I that I should develop my archery, and on most days I contrived to put in some practice. As I grew taller so he increased the strength and size of my bow, making it always so that its length exceeded my own height by at least a foot. This, he said, was the true long bow, the cheapest, the finest, and the deadliest of all weapons.

The time came when I could outmatch Tom, both in accuracy and speed. And this gave him pleasure, for although his shoulders now were often stiff with rheumatism, he declared that this mattered nothing since he had bestowed on me all the old skills of his hand and eye.

I do not say it vainly, but in those years I became a very good bowman. There was a particular trick of archery I learned, and it was this: whilst Tom counted sixty, I would shoot off a score of arrows, and on my nimblest days I would have five arrows in the air at the same instant, and every arrow would fall near to my chosen mark at a hundred paces distant. Such shooting is a matter of practice and good teaching, and there never was a better teacher of the bow than Tom.

But I have said that these were not entirely happy years. In fact, our homeland of the Lakes was under almost continual harassment by Count Ralf in the east, with an army based on Ambleside; and in the west, by the mercenaries of his younger brother, William Meschin. True we suffered no grievous loss, but yet at times we were sore contained, gripped as it were by the jaws of a monstrous pair of pincers.

We had never troubled much about Count William for he rarely troubled us. His lands lay well to the north, the flat, green lands towards the Scottish border. But now the two brothers were working more astutely together, and whilst Ralf ordered forays and assaults to be mounted from his side, William pushed aggressively southward down the western coast. Maryport and Moresby, those little ports we relied upon for trade with Ireland, Man, and Wales, swiftly fell to him. Then he advanced on that greater port which the Romans named Clanoventa, and which we called Ravenglass.

At this time, when I was barely fifteen, I was recruited into the army, and sent with five hundred other men and youths to the west. God knows, I was sad to leave Tom; yet I wanted to go, to fight, to scatter Count William to the winds with all his ravaging army!

Alas, I was not allowed my bow, but was given instead a sword and shield, and told to march. We marched all one day, and all night, with but a few hours' rest, and as we descended the heights of Scarfell, we met refugees from Ravenglass and Barnscar, and saw flames and smoke rising from the burning buildings. It almost broke my heart.

We tarried three days, hoping that Count William might advance into the fells, where we would have indulged in a great and bloody killing. But he was too wily a bird to be trapped like that; and so at last we marched back whence we had come, without shooting one arrow or unsheathing a single sword.

The loss of Ravenglass, though bitter, was not a fatal blow. Our ships traded furtively, using small, unguarded anchorages on moonless nights. And, as chance would have it, Count William progressed no further, for tidings came that the Scots were pressing his northern lands and threatening to invest Carlisle. So he withdrew much of his army, yet contriving to leave two or three well-armed garrisons on the coast.

Another hard blow befell us when the site of one of our best silver mines, far to the east beyond Hartside Height, was betrayed to Count Ralf. A dozen miners were captured, and those who would not slave for Ralf were put to death. Of this event I knew nothing at the time. I went back to the fells, and there, under the wide heavens, I felt secure.

Even had I known about the silver mine, I would not have understood that loss of silver meant loss of trade, and that loss of trade meant loss of arms and armour. My young mind was engrossed with sheep and bows and arrows, and the dales and mountains which I loved for the sense of security they gave me.

I loved them in all their moods: gay in the springtime with the gorse like golden fire above the bluebell mists; gentle in summer, with the hills immense and close, and the calm lakes glittering, and bees humming in the heather; mysterious in autumn when the peaks are remote and dreaming in the clouds; majestic and savage in winter whiteness with the north wind crying in the crags. At nights I would lie on my bed of bracken listening to the silence that is not really a silence at all. For as you listen you realise countless tiny sounds: a sighing of a breeze, a tinkling of water, a rustling of grasses, the turning of a leaf by some tiny, scurrying creature. There is always something; and it is like a breathing of the fellsides all around you.

Sometimes in the pitch darkness of winter, I would hear the screaming of a vixen for her mate, and I would curse her for she menaced our sheep. And sometimes I would hear the forlorn crying of flying geese beneath the cold, bright stars, and I would bless them, for they are pretty, harmless creatures, and they fly bravely to far away places.

I remember how the first year of a new century came in with great cold and mighty blizzards, and how Tom and I were desperate in those dark days for our poor sheep. With the spring came a great thaw and the becks and burns became wild rivers, stepping stones and bridges were swept away, and many a lambing ewe was drowned. We had barely finished counting our losses when, on a morning of early summer, I was summoned to the Manor House. The messenger could not, or would not, tell me why I was wanted, only that I must attend on Earl Bueth immediately.

I bade farewell to Tom and set out in good spirits on the long march across the fells. But little by little a sense of foreboding came into me. What could he want with me, that gaunt old man whose frail body was a mockery of manhood? With every step I became more uneasy, remembering the hardness of his tongue, and the strange, compelling power of his eyes.

I reached the Manor House late in the afternoon. It seemed to me exactly as it had been four years earlier: many people passing to and fro and all indifferent to me; a great fire crackling in the centre of the room; and beyond the fire, the solitary, white-haired old man, hunched in his great chair on the platform, and the two yellow hounds at his feet. I went forward and knelt.

"Stand," said he.

I did so and he sat for a long time without speaking. I could feel his eyes probing me, and I clenched my hands at my back and returned his stare.

"A puny sort of hawk," said he. And he put forth a hand and clawed me closer.

"A shepherd boy," said he. "You have the looks of one, and the stench of one! Dare I trust you?"

"Yes, lord," said I.

"You said once that you would serve me faithfully—remember, boy?"

"Yes, lord."

"So say you! But what is in your heart? Is it love of us, of England, and hatred for that usurping Norman brood? Or is it—merely sheep?"

"They killed my brother, lord."

"So you remember? And what besides? Can you still say your prayers in Latin and get your tongue round those strange French words?"

"Yes, lord."

"But you are a shepherd boy! Your heart is given to old Tom and the flocks up there on the fells."

"Yes, lord."

He was silent for some moments. Then said he:

"You are not going back there."

He cracked his knuckles, and thrust his face very close to mine. "You are not going back to the sheep, Alan. You are going on a long journey."

"What—what journey, lord?"

"To Winchester, the home of the Red King! That is where you are going, and you are going alone. What says your heart to this?"

I looked at him with a sort of horror in me. I thought of Tom, whom I loved, and my sheep, whom I loved, and the blue skies and the abiding peace of the fells. After some moments, I answered:

"Lord, if you say so, it is so."

He dropped back in his chair.

"These are hard times for us, Alan," he said, speaking now very softly. "And the worst is yet to come. Did you know that Count Ralf has been created Earl of Carlisle and is no longer in these parts? It is reported to me that he left two weeks ago and even now may be at Winchester. And I ask myself, why does he go there, what business takes him? It is in my mind that with his present army he cannot succeed against us. But if Rufus helps him with men or money, if he can recruit a bigger army, he will come against us more fiercely than before, and overwhelm us if he can. You understand?"

"I understand, lord. But what am I to do at Winchester?"

"Men talk, they always talk. You will watch, you will listen. If Ralf is recruiting a new army, you will soon know of it. Learn all you can, then come back and report to us."

I asked: "When do I start, lord?"

"Tomorrow. You will go by way of Earith, which is close to Ely in the land of Fens. Hereward, whose land that was, sold himself to the Bastard long ago, but you will find Wilfrid Leifson, his kinsman there, still fighting for the old liberties, as we do. Wilfrid will shelter you, and you will ask him to help us with money, or with men, or both. Tonight you will lodge with Benedict and by first light you can be on your way. Now listen, listen carefully . . ."

And thus he instructed me for another hour.

Beginning a Journey 6

I REACHED Father Benedict's house in the thickening dusk. A sturdy little horse in the field adjoining ran up to me, whinnying loudly, and I paused to fondle it. Then Father Benedict called, and I saw him darkly outlined in the candlelit doorway. "Come in, come in, Alan," he said kindly. "I expected you earlier. You have had a long interview with Earl Bueth. Come in, supper is ready."

I followed him inside. In the past four years I had seen very little of him; and now, as the pale wash of candlelight fell full upon him, he seemed smaller than I remembered him, and his eyes held an infinite sadness. A shyness overcame me, so that I scarcely knew what to say to him.

He put a dish of rabbit before me, and spoke grace, his eyes closed and his head bowed. And I, looking through my fingers, saw a travelling cloak and a leather bag, and a saddle and bridle on a stool, gleaming bright beside the fire. And that set me thinking, for since Earl Bueth had instructed me to travel light and on foot, with only my knife for protection, and a water bottle and a purse of silver pennies for my baggage, I knew those things could not be for me.

Father Benedict inquired kindly about my work on the fells, with never a word of blame for the disappointment I had been to him, though always with that deep sadness in his eyes. And presently, he said; "And you are returning to Tom in the morning, my son?"

"No, Father," I said. "I am not going back."

"How is that?" he asked, with a little upward flick of his eyebrows. "Where are you going, then?"

"Didn't my lord tell you, Father?"

"He sent word only that he wished you to sleep here tonight

and that you must be astir at first light. Where are you going, Alan?"

"I—I am going an errand, Father."

"An errand? Where to?"

"To—to Scotland," I said.

It was a wild lie. But I had to say something, for Earl Bueth had sworn me to secrecy, and this direct questioning had taken me by surprise. Father Benedict did not speak, but I had the feeling that he knew that I was lying, and I piled lie upon lie to convince him I was speaking the truth, making up a tale that I had to carry an order for swords to a Scotch armourer living on the Solway. Under his calm scrutiny I became more and more confused in my story, and at last, since he still did not speak, I pointed to the harness and bag and cloak by the fireside, exclaiming: "And you're travelling too, I see, Father."

"To Penrith, my son," he said. "I am called to the Abbey for a month."

"A month!" said I. "Why are you going for so long?"

"For the good of my soul," he answered simply. "To pay penance for my sins." And while I was wondering what sins of his could justify a month of penance, he added, "Since you're going north, too, let us travel together."

"I haven't a horse," I said quickly.

"You can travel on mine. She's a strong little beast, she'll carry the pair of us quite easily."

I had no answer for that.

After supper I pleaded my tiredness and the necessity of rising early, and retired to my room. The scent of the new-cut bracken on which I lay was sharp in my nostrils, my mind was wracked with nameless anxieties, and I thought I should never sleep. But I must have done. After a time I thought I saw Father Benedict bending over me, his lids drooping over his dark, sad eyes, and his small hands held over me almost as if in prayer, but swinging from his right hand was a length of rope.

I roused and sat up with a cry. And I saw that I was alone.

I did not sleep after that. In an hour or so I rose and went outside where the moonlight lay like a spread of snow over land and lake. I stripped and washed myself all over in the lake, and came out shivering, and ran and jumped on the bank to warm and dry myself. All the time I was trying to think how I could excuse myself from going into Penrith with Father Benedict. I still felt, illogically, that he knew my true errand was not to Scotland.

But I could think of no excuse. When at last I returned to the house, breakfast was ready. It occurred to me to plead that I felt sick and could not travel, but a moment's reflection told me that I would never deceive the good Father with such a tale.

Over the eastern hills the sky had lightened with a pink flush which was reflected in the serene waters of the lake. Father Benedict swallowed his bread, spoke a prayer, then passed me my water bottle and took up his cloak and bag and went outside, telling me to bring the harness. I heard him coaxing the mare from the field, then he shouted my name twice, rather impatiently. I took up the harness and went out to him.

He threw the saddle on to the horse's back, then put on the bridle. "Come, Alan," said he briskly, as I stood by, mute and unhelpful. "What's amiss this morning? It's high time we were on our way."

I did not move. The tip of the sun showed in a cleft of the hills and lit up the lake in a swift golden burst. And at the same time a pair of magpies flew from a spinney by the lake's edge with a loud whirring of wings, and landed close by, crying *Chacka-chacka-chak!* They moved towards us all unsuspecting in a hoppy, jaunty walk, then seeing us, rose with a screech, and vanished into the trees. And there flashed into my mind a fable old Tom had told me of, and in my desperation, I seized on it.

"It's an omen!" I cried.

Father Benedict looked up from fastening the saddle. "An omen? What do you mean by that?"

"The pies, Father! When they chatter like that it's dead men talking! They are demon birds, they have eaten the flesh of men! Oh, it's bad luck, Father."

"The pies are God's creatures as we are, Alan. Come, it's time we were moving."

He was standing by the horse, ready to mount.

"I'm not coming," I said.

"It's an old woman's tale you tell me, my son," he replied

calmly. "I've taught you better than to believe such things. Here, take the rein, I'll ride behind you. It's pleasanter in front."

He held the rein out to me. I stepped away from him with a little flutter of fear moving in me. For in that moment I saw him exactly as I had visualised him in my vision of the night, except that then he had held not a rein but a rope.

He would have spoken, but I said again loudly:

"I'm not coming, Father."

He looked at me in silence, with the sadness of all the world upon him. At last he said simply: "God be with you, Alan," and he mounted, and rode away.

The mocking chatter of the magpies burst out at him as he passed the spinney. He turned once in the saddle to look back at me, then rode steadily forward.

I watched him until he was lost from sight beyond the trees, then I set off on the narrow track to the south, where lay the land of Fens; and far beyond that, Winchester, capital of the Red King.

7 Setchel Fen

I STOOD ON the eminence called Cupar's Hill and looked upon the desolation of the Fens.

To the north was forest, black against a white and solid sky that shone like the inside of an oyster shell. There, too, lay wolds where sheep and cattle grazed, falling gently to fens which showed green here, where you could tread safe and even ride a horse, and brown there, where you would be sucked down for certain unless you knew the secret paths. And laced through the fens was the bright, white water: brooks and streamlets and river reaches, and great smooth lakes where waterfowl clacked and honked and hooted. Except for those gentle uplands in the north, all was flatness. And even on this summer's day, the hissing wind from the east cut at you like a scythe. They say men find a spirit of freedom in the Fenland such as they find nowhere else in England. But to me, brought up in the comforting shadow of mountains, it is the freedom of a wilderness.

Although my journey had been somewhat eased by Earl Bueth's purse of pennies, which I carried on a belt beneath my tunic, it had been a long, hard march to the Fens. And now I was here I had to find the camp of Wilfrid, for Earl Bueth had never been there, and could not direct me precisely. It seemed to me, as I looked down from the slopes of Cupar's Hill, that I might seek Wilfrid for years and years in this fenland desolation and never find him.

First, then, I went into Ely, a bustling town to my bewildered eyes, where many Frenchmen, and Englishmen, too, laboured on the building of the great cathedral. I put sly questions to these men; they talked freely of Hereward—and why should they not, for that Lord of Bourne in the end had become the

Bastard's creature!—but when I spoke of Wilfrid, they shrugged their shoulders and smiled wryly, and some there were who swore and raised their fists at me.

So I came from Ely and headed for Aldreth where Hereward had once made his stand. But now all was deserted there, overgrown with nettle, sedge, and bramble. I saw the wide Ouse lazily westering, and with a sort of desperation in me I decided to follow it, and now at last my good angel Gabriel marched with me. Near the hamlet of Earith I fell in with an old, one-eyed peat-cutter named John, who was glad to employ me, for he was such a drunken rascal that he could get none to labour for him. In return for food and shelter in his hut, I drove a wagon load of peat into Ely every day, and sometimes twice a day.

John's favoured drink was a rough mead which he made himself from the honey of wild bees. He boasted that he had been a follower of Hereward; and one night, when he was very tipsy, I egged him on to relate some stories of his youth, and then I whispered the name of Wilfrid to him. He put a thick brown finger to his lips and screwed his one eye into a wink.

"Wilfrid," said he, "Ah, *him*.! . . . They'll take him and gibbet him, they will. They'll slice out his guts for him—zip, zap, like that! Seen it done many a time, I have."

I filled the old man's cup. "They say Wilfrid's camp is hereabouts," I said.

He drank noisily. Then he placed an arm round my shoulder, and drew me to him, and put his lips to my ear.

"Along Setchel Fen, there's where," said he. And with his thumb nail he sketched on the earthen floor: the fen, the river, an island on which he stabbed his thumb. "Thar—thar's Wilfrid."

I asked: "How can you reach there?"

"No ways," old John said. "No ways 'cept by boat, and you ha'n't a boat, ha' you?"

"No, I haven't a boat, master," I said.

In the early hours, with the Great Bear standing overhead, I left John snoring with his head tucked into his elbow, and went down to the fen.

In the dark it was a place for demons. Every tree and every

bush loomed monstrous. This was the deep fen and I went warily, prodding my way with a willow wand. Presently I came to a band of gently moving water, and I followed it until I reached a drooping, dripping willow. Beneath the tree were moored three boats, with fowlers' nets and lines in one of them. I took the smallest boat and pushed out into the stream.

I allowed the boat to drift for several minutes before I put out the oars. There was nothing to be heard except the creak of the oars and the soft swish-swish of the water against the boat. When at last I thought I must be nearing Setchel Fen, I ran for the cover of some tall reeds. Soon the sky lightened, the outline of the reeds sharpened, three ducks went darkly winging overhead. At the first strike of the sun I saw, far over to my left, an island; and that, thought I, must be Wilfrid's island.

I pulled across to it, running for a sheltered, reedy place where the sunlight fell bright and warm. It was a hard pull, farther than I had reckoned, but at last I ran into the shallows and secured the boat and dropped breathless into the long grass. It was wonderfully peaceful, and I saw nothing to indicate that this was the stronghold of an English rebel.

Perhaps, after all, I had made a mistake. I stepped towards a clump of alder trees; then, suddenly, I stopped. For there had come to me (and I know not how it came) the certain knowledge that I was being watched.

Then I saw the child's face peering through the tall sedge grass. At first I thought it was a boy; but when she raised her head, I saw the dark plaits on her shoulders and knew her for a girl.

"Who are you?" I asked. She rose to her knees, staring, full of sulky suspicion. "Who are you?" I asked again, and she answered simply:

"Patrice."

"Do you live here?"

"What does it matter to you where I live?"

"It doesn't matter," I said.

She looked coldly at me. Then she asked: "Where do you come from? What's your name?"

"I'm Alan of Lakeland," I said.

"Where's Lakeland?"

"In the north. A long way from here."

"What are you doing here?"

"I have a message for Wilfrid. Do you know him?"

"No, I don't know him."

"I'm sure you do," I said.

"All right, I do."

"How well do you know him?"

"He's my father."

"Then you can take me to him!"

She rose slowly to her feet. She was a tall, thin girl of perhaps thirteen, bare-armed and bare-legged in a drab dress reaching to her knees. She was pretty with a strange, wan prettiness: her face was small and sallow, her chin pointed and wilful, her eyes brown as the bat's wing. She looked like a child witch.

"Where is Wilfrid?" I asked.

"Why should I tell you?"

"Because . . ."

"Oh, because of a message, you say! That's a lie!"

"It isn't a lie!"

"Prove it! Prove you're not telling lies!"

I went up to her and gripped her arms. She tightened her lips, but she did not flinch or yield a step. I said firmly: "Take me to your father, girl. I have come a long way to see him."

She gave a quick laugh and wriggled away.

"All right, I'll take you. Come on!"

She danced off up the bank and through some trees. "Come on!" she called. "Come on, what's keeping you?" And she darted on again. I lost her beyond a thick bush of furze, and when next I saw her she was forty yards away. "Come on, boy!" she called, and laughed her quick, shrill laugh. And with her laughter, I heard movement in the brushwood behind me, and I turned, knowing she had tricked me. A blow on my head knocked me to the ground, and as I struggled to rise a hand seized me by the hair, I felt a cold edge of steel against my throat, and a man's voice snarled:

"If tha knows what's good, be still. I'll slit tha gizzard else."

I knew what was good, and lay quite still.

8 Patrice

I FELT MORE angry than frightened; angry with the girl for fooling me, angry with myself for being fooled. The man's puckered dark eyes contemplated me in silence for some moments, then said he: "Who is tha?"

"He's a spy, Amos!" the girl piped. "He came in a boat, out of the mists from Earith—I saw!"

"A spy, is tha?" the man said slowly, still with his knife against my throat.

"Don't heed her!" I cried. "Take me to Wilfrid. It's important, I swear!"

"We'll see if tha's a spy or nay," the man said. And he jerked me up by the hair, and turned me about, and forced me forward at a sharp run. I glimpsed the shapes of men and women, I heard shouts. We reached a clearing where stood brushwood huts. The man pitched me into one of them, kicking my buttocks as I fell. I hit the floor with a force that wrenched a groan from me; and there I lay, gasping for breath, until presently strong hands lifted me. I dragged the [illegible] from my eyes and saw half a dozen men about me, and I felt suddenly stupid and ashamed. One of the party, a tall, grave, grey-haired man, took me by the chin and looked long at my face.

"Is this the best the French can do for a spy?"

Nobody answered him, nor did he seem to expect an answer. "Fetch me a stool," he said; and when they fetched it, he sat, leaning forward, his long fingers gripping his knees. "Come, Patrice," he said, and the girl came forward from the doorway, a sulky look on her pale face, and stood beside him.

"So the villain came in a boat?"

"Yes, father."

"Alone?"

"Yes, father."

"And he spied on us?"

"Oh, no!" she answered pertly. "I never gave him the chance."

"But he *would* have spied on us but for you?"

"Of course! What else does he want here?"

"What else, indeed!" the man said. And to me: "I am Wilfrid whom you wish to see. Are you satisfied, boy?"

"The girl's a fool," I protested. "I am not a spy! I have been sent by my lord, the Earl Bueth."

"That's a pretty tale! How do I know it's true?"

"I tell you so, sir."

"Aye, I hear it," he said, snapping a thumb. "I would hear it just as plain if you told me you came from the Sun or the Moon! Did not Earl Bueth give you some token to bring to me?"

"No, sir." Then, at a thought, I added quickly: "But he gave me a purse of pennies which I have with me."

"Let me see your purse of pennies," he said.

I took the purse from beneath my tunic and gave it to him. He emptied the pennies into the palm of one hand, then slid them slowly back into the purse. "Ten pennies. That's quite a fortune for a boy. Take care you don't lose them." He threw the purse back to me. "Let us suppose your name is Alan and that you come from Earl Bueth of the Lakes. Now tell me more."

I told him of our struggle in the Lakes: how William Meschin had captured the western ports, and Ralf Meschin had seized the best of our silver mines; and that though we had no thought of giving up the struggle, we were sore pressed and needed help.

"And what help does Earl Bueth expect of me?"

"We want men, sir. We want arms and money."

He was silent for a little, biting on his lip. Then said he, with almost savage bitterness:

"Boy, your Earl Bueth is an old falcon who lives in the clouds and does not see what passes here below! He does not know that we are a pitiful few, a beggarly garrison beset on all sides by the enemy, so that our fortress island is no better than a prison! He does not know that our gold is spent, that our arms are old, or that in this hot summer the waters which surrounded us have fallen and fallen, so that at any time the Frenchmen may cross the fens and attack! On moonless nights we are contriving to slip away from here in ones and twos, and if God grant us grace for a couple of months, they will find all the birds have flown when they come. Meanwhile, those of us who are left have only fish to feed us, for we have no sheep or cattle, and the Frenchmen have driven the waterfowl down river beyond our reach. Why, I'd give a fortune, if I had it, for a dozen of your Lakeland sheep and a wagonload of flour! That's how it stands with us, Alan of the Lakes, and you must go back to your Earl Bueth, with my love and English greeting, and tell him as I tell you."

He put his hand on my shoulder, and added in a kinder tone:

"I'm truly sorry, Alan. We would help you if we could. I know that whatever happens to us here, you will go on fighting in the north, for that is the sort of people you are. And perhaps in time some of us will march north and join with you. Let us pray for that."

I stood speechless, not knowing what to say. But looking shyly now at Wilfrid's face, and the faces of those about him, it seemed to me that they all had the pallid skin and bright-eyed look that denotes hunger, and I thought of a way in which I might help them.

I asked: "Where are the nearest sheep to here?"

The question put them at a loss. But after some moments, one answered: "There are the sheep of Jehan l'Estrange eight miles down river beyond the Axham Mill."

To Wilfrid, I said: "Sir, if you can give me a long bow and a dozen arrows, I'll get some sheep."

He smiled at that. "So you're a bowman, boy?"

"I'll outshoot any of your men," said I.

"Fetch him a bow and arrows," Wilfrid said.

They fetched me a good bow a hand's width taller than myself. The arrows were not so good as I could have made, but they would serve well enough. I refused Wilfrid's offer to send a man to Axham Mill with me, for the weight of another in the boat would scarcely have left room for the carcasses of sheep. After some reflection, however, I asked that he would have a light burning two nights hence by the alder trees, where I had first landed.

"Patrice will be there with a lantern," he promised. And when the girl stood silent, he added sharply: "You hear, Patrice?"

She answered sulkily: "Yes, father."

I set out in the boat an hour after dusk. All about me was deep darkness. It was eerie there on the broad river; the night birds crying from the distant banks seemed to mock at me from another world. I love the twilight and the darkness, but this was a darkness foreign to me, and I felt terribly alone. I rowed blindly on and on; several times I became fast on mudbanks, and had to jump overboard to push the boat free, standing waist-deep in the water. My progress in consequence was slow; but at long last the stars overhead were blotted out by a building uprearing in the darkness; and I knew from what Wilfrid's men had told me that this must be Axham Mill, and that the sheepfold lay just beyond.

I pulled into the rushes and lay hidden all that day, plagued by the midges and listening to the muffled rattling of the mill-wheel. With the first shades of dusk, I took up my bow and half a dozen arrows, waded to the bank, and slithered on my belly into the pasture.

I could see a brace of sheep a hundred paces off. The ground sloped up gently and I heard more sheep beyond the crest of the hillock. I thought, too, that I could hear a man's voice. I crept forward, and from the top of the slope I looked down upon a fine flock of fifty or more cropping at the lush herbage. A breeze was blowing from the river, so that I lay to windward of them, and I feared they must soon scent me. I crept closer. I could see nothing of the shepherd. Twilight deepened fast, the nearest sheep became dim blobs in the gloom. I dared not delay any longer.

I crept forward again. When I was fifty paces from a knot of four sheep, I thrust four arrows into the ground before me. Then I rose and let fly. Nock, aim, loose; one, two, three, four. The arrows sped almost as fast as that. Death came to those creatures so swiftly and so kindly out of the summer's night that they knew nothing of it. With the grass still in their jaws they dropped, as if overcome by a charm of sleep.

It took me a long time to get the carcasses down to the boat.

I could drag only one at a time and I moved with great stealth, for although I now had the shelter of darkness, I feared lest the shepherd and his dog might be near, and hear me.

I had hoped to be back at Wilfrid's island before the night was out. But now I had not only to row blindly into the darkness, but I had the added weight of the sheep, and the current of the stream to contend with. I lost count of the times I ran on to mudbanks. When the pink flush of morning came to the river, I was still far from the island, and I had to lay up all that day amongst the reeds.

At dusk I rowed on again. The night seemed to fold itself about me like a curtain. Again and again, thinking I must be near the island, I looked across my shoulder, hoping to see the glimmer of a lantern at the landing place. I was a whole day later than I had planned to be; but this I thought would make no difference, and Patrice would be there to welcome me and guide me in.

Suddenly I saw that I was running past the island, and I had to put about quickly in mid-stream, with a deal of swirling and splashing. I came into the landing place very quietly, and rested there upon the oars listening. There was no light, no sound, no movement of any kind. The scent of woodsmoke came down to me on the wind.

I went ashore and walked slowly along the narrow path to the camp. Presently I saw a thin glowing line of fire ahead of me, and my heart seemed to stop as I ran forward.

I reached the clearing. There was nothing left of Wilfrid's camp; nothing except a smouldering heap of ashes. In the centre of the clearing a great funeral pyre burned over several bodies. I stood there staring, telling myself it wasn't true, it couldn't be true. The ashes of the pyre gleamed white and purple-blue, and tiny jigging flames seemed to deride me with a crackling laughter. I stood staring, and I knew that it must be true, that at last the French had struck and gallant Wilfrid's resistance was at an end.

I walked back down the winding path, back into the blessed darkness, feeling sick and faint. I sat by the boat, trying to realise what had happened and to piece my scattered thoughts together. Presently I heard a soft sighing moan in the darkness; and I searched amongst the bushes and brushwood beyond the alder trees. There I found Patrice lying senseless on her back, a broken horn lantern at her side.

I put my face close to hers. She gave no sign that she saw me. I spoke her name. She did not stir. Then I saw that my left hand was dark with her blood, and I found the wound, a great gaping sword cut high up on her right thigh.

I returned to the camp and found there a cracked dish which I filled with water, and I gave Patrice a little to drink and washed her wound.

She said nothing, she did not stir. But I felt that she was aware of me and what I was doing. I was glad now of the medical lore I had learned long ago from Father Benedict. With daylight I collected some good clean moss, and from the breast of one of the sheep carcasses, I cut off some fine white fat; and from these two I concocted an unguent with which I covered the girl's wound and bound it on tightly with long flat leaves of reed mace.

All that morning she lay quietly, and every so often I made her sip water from the dish.

Late in the afternoon four mounted Frenchmen returned to the island. I saw them a long way off, picking their path carefully across the fen. Then they put their horses to the river, and in mid-stream the horses had to swim a little. They came ashore at the distant end of the island. I had no doubt these men had returned to ensure that none of Wilfrid's followers had escaped the massacre, and I took up my bow and stood in the cover of the alder trees, determined that they should die if they approached us.

But they never came. After an hour or so I saw them recrossing the river, and I thought what fine sturdy steeds they had, and how good it would be to possess a horse to carry me from this accursed place.

With the possibility that they might return again, I did not dare to remain on the island. When evening came, I tossed three of the sheep carcasses into the river and carried Patrice down to the boat. She had gained wonderfully in strength and made some feeble protest that she would not leave. I told her sharply to hold her tongue, and pulled over to the wooded south bank of the river. There, in the shelter of a birch spinney, we spent the night.

Patrice slept soundly. In the morning she could stand and even hobble about a little. But her dark mood persisted, and again and again she demanded to be taken back to the island. She could tell me little about the raid, saying that the French had attacked in the evening mists just after she had set out with the lantern for the landing place. A man on a horse had cut her down and left her for dead; even now she did not know what had happened at the main camp. I told her that it was a place of death and ashes, and that I felt sure none but she had escaped.

She wept at that and was silent.

Then I said: "Patrice, if the Frenchmen find us, they will certainly kill us. You can't go back to the island, nor can you stay here. I am going south and you must come with me."

She screwed up her small face in a spasm of anger and yelled: "I won't come! I won't come!"

But already I had formed a rough and ready plan. It would be madness to remain here an hour longer than we had to, for if the enemy suspected our presence, they would certainly hunt us down. And again I thought how fine it would be to possess a horse.

Earl Bueth had been against that, saying that a peasant boy on a horse would create notice. But now I could only reflect how quickly a horse would carry us away from our present perils. I had not money to buy a horse and therefore I would have to steal one. I knew that I must summon up all my courage and act quickly.

In the full light of morning I rowed over to the north bank of the river, then took a path across the fen, and so came to a road. I could see hoofmarks in the dust, and, commending myself to Gabriel and to God, I followed them. After a long walk I reached a hamlet, and beyond the hamlet a fine house with a dovecote and big stables. In the stable yard, three horses were cropping at a truss of hay which a groom had spread before them.

There was nobody in the yard. The horses were quite free, not fastened in any way. I waited, possessed by a sudden stark fear that turned my stomach to water. I counted seven times seven to still the frenzied hammering of my heart; but it would not be stilled. So I clenched my teeth and walked into the yard, and took up the rein of the nearest horse, a lovely little sorrel mare.

Unlike the others she lacked a saddle but carried a blanket over her back loosely fastened with a surcingle. A water bottle and a satchel containing bread and meat had been put down by the mounting block. I picked them up. Nobody called, nobody came. I led the mare outside to the wide grass verge beyond the road. I mounted and gave her a hard slap across the neck and kicked my heels into her sides.

She went away like the wind.

She was sweating when we reached the river. I put her straight into the water and I felt her quiver at the shock. But she had a heart as big as herself and did not falter; and so in my mind I called her Fearless. Soon we were across the river and safe within the spinney. Patrice limped forward and looked at me tight-lipped.

"We've got a horse," I said cheerfully. "Rest while you can. We shall journey south tonight."

"I won't come, I won't come!" she cried.

I argued long with her. But she would only screech at me, like some crazy caged bird, "I won't come! I won't, I won't, I won't!" At last I left her and made myself a bed in long grass at the other end of the spinney; and I did not stir until late afternoon, when I watered Fearless and bridled her. With some misgiving, I discarded the bow Wilfrid had given me, for I could not conceal it, and I thought it too dangerous to carry openly.

The sun went down, river mists rose and thickened. I said to Patrice: "Are you ready?"

"I won't come!"

"They'll kill you else," said I, moving to take her hand.

"Take me back to the island!" she screamed.

"You are a fool, Patrice," I said.

She flung herself at me, her thin hands clawed like talons. "Bastard boy! Bastard! Bastard!" I seized her wrist and she fastened her teeth so deep in my hand that the blood spurted. I threw her down, but she was up in an instant. I mounted Fearless, and as she came to attack again, I gave her a kick that sent her sprawling.

She lay there panting, grimacing with surprise and pain. Slowly she rose to her knees.

"Bastard boy!" she sobbed, and spat at me.

"Stay, you witch's whelp!" I shouted in an anger as wild as hers. "Stay and die, it's all you deserve!"

And I rode off through the trees.

Beyond the spinney a track led to a road that ran due south. Away from the river, the air was clear and the stars showed sharp and bright, the self-same stars that shone upon the lakes and hills of home. They gave me direction, but more than this, they gave me comfort, a sense of being seen and guarded by a thousand friendly eyes.

That night I made good progress, keeping to open heathlands where I could, and avoiding the villages and towns. When the first grey streaks of dawn showed in the eastern sky, I made for the shelter of a wood, and there I watered and tethered my good Fearless, and settled down to sleep.

But I could not sleep. Again and again my thoughts turned to Patrice; I seemed to hear the shrill insistence of her voice, and to see the wan and angry little face.

They would find her soon, I thought. They would slit her throat and disembowel her, and leave her for the rats and ravens.

And it would serve her right.

I must have dozed for a few hours. When I awoke it was almost dark. At once I thought again of Patrice, and I knew I must go back.

I could not leave her to that foul death.

I mounted Fearless and turned north. It was hard going, for now a vast drape of cloud covered my friendly stars and at times I could scarcely see beyond the mare's ears. When at last I struck the birch spinney and saw the river shining white through the trees, it was broad daylight.

I dismounted and led Fearless to the old encampment.

Patrice was lying there like one already dead, her head pillowed on her thin arms, her face turned away from me.

Suddenly she stirred. She saw me and gave a soft, meaningless cry. Then she rose and clutched at me, wailing so piteously that I could not understand her words. But presently she drew a long deep breath, and sobbed: "Let me come, Alan—oh, let me come with you!"

"Come—if you'll behave," I answered roughly. But my heart was full of gladness.

We set off at eventide, she sitting behind me on the little mare's haunches, with her arms very tight about my waist.

Winchester 9

MANY DAYS later (I do not know how many, for I did not count them) we came suddenly to Winchester. It is a great city, this Venta Belgarum of the Romans, with a church so vast that you can scarcely see from one end of it to the other. But the town lies in a sort of basin or deep hollow of the chalk hills, and you are on it almost before you are aware.

We had travelled without trouble or incident. Two days after leaving the Fens I felt it safe to move in daylight; and so we travelled fast along the old roads and ancient trackways, clinging to the uplands where we could, and avoiding the morass of that fearful forest named Anderida, which is fit, men say, only for wolves and swine and brigands.

Thus we came down from Basing, seeing the play of cloud shadows across the swelling hills before us, and the oxen dragging the wagons, and the sheep and the kine browsing. Then suddenly the hills opened out and we saw the City of the Red King nestling darkly beneath us, and the great church, and the mill and the river, and the wagons and the numberless people moving to and fro; and we stopped in wonder.

Winchester is a walled city; you make your way in and out of it through five main gates. We watched a fat woman waddling along the road, leading a fat pig by a rope through a ring in its nose. Then a wagoner went before us, his cart stacked with vegetables for market, and I decided to follow him to the West Gate.

Patrice and I had concocted a story that we were brother and sister, and had come to Winchester seeking news of our father, an armourer in the service of Ralf, Earl of Carlisle. But I had no wish to be questioned if I could avoid it; for as old Tom used to say, the fewer lies you tell, the less chance is there of being found out.

We pushed on until we were close behind the wagoner, and there we held our distance. The West Gate stood wide open, and I saw a guard or sentinel on duty beneath the arch, and I thought that now we were bound to be questioned. And so we should have been but for the accident of the woman with the pig.

The pig must have heard the rumble of the wagon behind it and taken fright, for it darted away with a fearful squealing, and the poor woman, attempting to grab the rope which had slipped from her hands, fell flat in the dust. We dismounted and I managed to catch the pig as it was running off over the fields, and brought it back to the woman who was lying in the road, with the guard from the gate bending over her.

She was a peasant woman, not so old as I had thought her, with a face as round and as rosy as an apple. Her dress was torn and there was blood on her hands and knees. Between us the guard and I lifted her on to the back of Fearless, and in this way we passed without hindrance into the city of Winchester, Patrice leading the mare, I leading the pig, and goodwife Mercy Asser (for this, she told us, was her name) sitting with her fat legs swinging and her fat arms folded across her dusty bosom.

We passed down the main city street, which slopes steeply to a bridge over the river, and is called Chepe Street. The goodwife smiled and waved her hand at some of her friends there, and I could not help reflecting that it was no bad thing that she had befriended us, too. Short of the East Gate we turned down an alley to the left; and there, just within the city walls, and close to the sparkling river, we came to a green space on which stood a hut built of rough-hewn timber. At the sound of our voices, four little half-naked children ran out, yelling, "Ma, Ma! Have you fetched the sow, Ma?"

This was the goodwife's home, and these were her children.

We helped her dismount, and Patrice, fetching some water from the river, bathed her scratches, whilst the children crowded round, full of noise and questions, though little concerned for their mother's accident.

She cuddled them, and told us that Asser, her husband, a

forester in the King's service, was away at Malwood, in the New Forest. I pricked up my ears at this, and would have questioned her, but she looked at me very direct with her pale blue eyes, saying:

"You are strangers to these parts, sure-lye?"

I admitted it.

"Then who might you be, young master?"

"We are orphans, we are brother and sister," Patrice said.

"We are the children of an armourer in the service of Ralf Meschin, Earl of Carlisle," I said. "I think milord is here in Winchester, is he not?"

"Yes, I've heard some speak of the Earl Ralf. What is your father's name?"

I was not prepared for this question, and could only stare stupidly at the woman. She smiled back, and turned to Patrice. "Well, my dear, what's your father's name? *You* have not forgotten, sure-lye?"

Patrice clasped her fingers tight and looked desperately at me. I spoke the first name that came to my lips.

"Garth."

"Garth," the woman said. "Garth, the armourer to milord Ralf. No, I haven't heard of this Garth."

I said lamely: "I—I am not sure our father is in Winchester."

"But if his master is here, where else should he be?"

"I don't know," I said.

The children were clamouring for food. The woman went into her hut to build up the fire, and we trooped in behind her. It was a dark and dirty hut consisting of but one room; hens and piglets ran in and out; the air smelt sour and foetid. Soon little flames danced in the fire embers and the smoke rose in a great blue feather to the sooted hole in the roof. The woman bent low over a blackened pot and stirred and stirred; and presently, skewering several chunks of meat on the point of a knife, she passed them to the children.

It was then that I became aware of another presence in the hut. As the flames lengthened and brightened, I saw an old woman hunched motionless on a stool at the far side of the room. Her face was as brown and as wrinkled as a nut; only her dark eyes moved, flicking this way and that, from the children to the goodwife, from the goodwife to Patrice and me. To me she seemed infinitely old, old beyond reckoning, old as the stars and mountains.

Goodwife Mercy saw me staring, and said: "Don't notice her."

"No," I said. But still I stared, she was so unbelievably old.

"It's Nell," the woman said. "She's Asser's grandam. She's a mad one. Don't notice her."

The children yelped and slobbered like a pack of puppies. The woman regarded them, smiling, then thrust a chunk of meat at Patrice, then at me. It was venison, a rich, dark meat—truly, thought I, a meat fit for a king! And it probably *was* the King's, a deer from the New Forest.

Patrice ate slowly, taking a little of the meat at a time between her thumb and fingers; and occasionally she would throw me a shy smile, and I knew she was content. For all her sharp and stubborn temper, she had a natural grace and the manners of good breeding. I saw the woman looking slyly at her as she fished up more meat for her ravenous children. Then, turning to me, she asked:

"Where be you lodging in Winchester, young master?"

"Could it be here?" said I.

She rounded her lips. "This is the way of it," she said, after a moment. "I launder linen from the castle, it's hard work, very hard, so it is. If your sister helps me with my work, I'll feed and lodge her, sure-lye."

"And me, goodwife?"

"Young master, I can't lodge you, truly I can't! I've not the room to lodge you, for Asser comes in from the forest most every sennight, and a hard-tempered one he is, and he'll beat me if I give you his space of the bed. Nay, I'll take your sister, I'll do that. You'll find lodgings easily enough in the town, look."

But she did not tell me where.

Now I was in a quandary. I did not care to leave Patrice in this hovel with the dirt and the yelling brats, and the hens and piglets, and the ancient hag in the shadows. But on the other hand I thought that here she would be well fed; and I felt there was nothing she needed in all the world so much as a week or two of solid feeding.

Lodging for myself was of no great importance. I could sleep as well in a ditch as in a bed—better in fact than in goodwife Mercy's bed which I did not doubt was full of fleas.

The woman agreed that Fearless could graze in the grassy stretch by her hut. We decided that Patrice should lodge with her for a few days at least—an arrangement which did not seem to please Patrice overmuch. But, as I told her, I believed it was for the best.

So I left her with goodwife Mercy and sought lodging at some houses near the main street of the town. But at none of them would they let me labour for my keep, and as the pennies in my purse had now dwindled to three, I was in no position to pay for lodging like a wealthy gentleman.

The day was well advanced and I wandered forlorn down to the river, watching the dragonflies skimming and hovering above the reeds like tiny fragments of a rainbow. With the dusk I went back to Fearless, and satisfied that she was comfortable and safely tethered, I carried away the blanket. A short distance east of the bridge, I came upon a boat supported on timber balks at the edge of a corn-field which ran down to the river. From its dryness I judged it had not been afloat for many months. I cut some reeds and spread them in the bottom of the boat, and on these I lay and covered myself with the blanket.

I watched the great hills darken, and a sickle moon rising, and the stars peep out one by one. I heard the night wind sweeping through the ripening corn, with a sound like the sea; and I recalled the lakes and streams and ghylls of home. I thought of my sheep, and old Tom; and with all my heart I wished that he was with me now, to soften my loneliness in this alien southern land of forests and green hills. I thought of the great man to whom I was pledged, Earl Bueth, and how I must use my wits to gain news of Count Ralf (always Count Ralf to me though he was Earl of Carlisle), and why Ralf had come to talk with the arch-tyrant Rufus when he had us so hard pressed in the fells; and what he planned for the future.

By what means I should learn these things I could not tell; but learn them I must, for that was the reason why I was sent here. And having learned them, I would hasten home and report to my lord; and perhaps soon he would lead us to victory in a great battle that would end all our battles, and I would settle content with my sheep and Tom, and never again would I leave them.

Thus my thoughts roamed as I lay snug in the boat, my eyes half closed. But suddenly I jerked up with a cry, knowing that I was not alone. The old crone, Nell, was kneeling beside me, her hands clawing the gunwale of the boat by my head. Even in the dark I could discern the lively dance of her eyes as she flashed them from stem to stern of the boat, from my face to my feet and back again.

"She aren't your sister," she muttered, husky as a crow.

I was sweating with the fright she had given me. But I took her meaning, and answered:

"She is, she's my sister."

"Nay, she aren't! You aren't like."

"I can't help that. She's my sister."

"Lies! Lies! The good Lord'll strike you down for such lies lest you take care, so he will! What's your name, what is it?"

"Alan."

"Where from, Alan?"

"Far away."

"She aren't your sister."

"Yes, she is."

"Garth aren't your father."

"Yes, he is."

"What's he like, Garth? Tall, short, fat, thin?"

"He—he's tall."

"How old, eh—how old?"

"I—I'm not sure."

"Moustaches?"

"Yes."

She cackled with laughter.

"Lies, lies—all lies. Garth aren't your father, nor she aren't your sister! I know it, and *she* knows—Mercy knows, though she don't say. She's a sly one, a bad one, that Mercy. Just you watch her, just take care!"

I was silent, not knowing how to answer her.

Her eyes flashed darkly. "Just take care, Alan," she said again. And she was gone.

It was a long time before I fell asleep.

Royal Scullion 10

I AWOKE REMEMBERING the crone. My immediate thought was that I must quickly find some other lodging for Patrice; but on reflection I realised that to take her away now would seem suspicious, and suspicion was the one thing I was anxious to avoid whilst my real business in Winchester was still in hand.

Trying to resolve my mind I walked several times up and down Chepe Street, which by some is called the King's Way. It is a street to amaze and bewilder, housing as it does the palace which the Bastard built, a great stone palace of many separate buildings, such as Castle, Mint, Stables, Chapel, and Treasury—which last, they say, is packed with gold, silver, and precious stones, looted from the homes of noble Englishmen. Hard by are the great Wool Market and factories for different kinds of workers, such as smiths, harness-makers, weavers, jewellers. There is also a street housing spear-makers and sword-makers, and another where labour the shield-makers. Truly, this Winchester is a place of many marvels.

As I say, I walked up and down Chepe Street until it struck me that if I went on in this way I must be noticed and wondered at; and I therefore took refuge in an alley on the south side of the street. It is strange indeed how Providence controls and guides us; had I gone down to the river and mused there, I would not have come to the decision that I did, and my story would probably have been very different.

On each side of the alley where I stood rose buildings of stone which are part of the great palace, and the air of the alley was heavy with the scent of meats and herbs. Here, obviously, were the kitchens, and it struck me at once that now was my opportunity to become part of the Red King's household, perhaps to have the run of rooms and passages in the palace. I would work in the royal kitchens, and for the time being Patrice must continue to lodge with the goodwife Mercy.

I went in through the arched doorway, and, descending some narrow steps, came into a great room, where the heat and the smells of cooking rose almost overpoweringly from the walls and the wide flagged floor. Everywhere cooks were busy, pounding, chopping, and cutting at benches, knives clattered, voices echoed, steam lifted from pots simmering over fires. Nobody took notice of me. I paused by a bench where two men were hacking at a sheep's carcass, and I said to one, a skinny, dark fellow: "Sir, if you please . . ."

"Be off with you," said he. But I was not to be put aside like that and stood my ground. His companion, a big, elderly, grey-headed man, looked over his shoulder, and said in French:

"What does the little monkey want, Jean?"

I answered at once, also in French: "Please, sir, the little monkey wishes to work for the King."

The big man stared, then threw his knife down on to the bench, and shook with soft laughter.

"Ho, you speak French, eh, my fellow? That's good, that's good! And you'd work with us, eh—eh?"

He ruffled my hair with his fat, blood-stained fingers, and laughing still, he took me aside. It was my luck that he was the under-chef of these great kitchens, and that my knowledge of French tickled him, and the glibness of my tongue convinced him that I wished for nothing so much as to learn from him the art of cooking. He called me a little monkey of a scullion, and in a few minutes I was dousing and cleansing a pile of platters in a stone basin in a corner.

I shall not here recall the details of my life as a royal scullion. It was a hard life in which I sometimes laboured from dawn to dawn with scarce a moment's respite. But when rest came I rested well, sometimes in a chamber off the kitchens with other scullions and cooks, sometimes in my boat by the river. There was always food to be had in plenty—too much food, too much grease, too much fine wine, too much drunkenness. The cooks were for the most part fat, besotted Frenchmen whom I held in scorn, though they treated me well enough. They did not interfere with me so long as the pots they gave me were decently scoured, or the vegetables washed, or the carcase bones scraped clean.

They did not trouble that I sometimes left them, and wandered off through the long underground passages to the dining hall, and many of the rooms and chambers, for I always made the pretence of being on some particular errand, such as collecting platters, or spreading rushes, or carrying a message. In this way I soon came to know my way about the palace fairly well.

Beneath the southern walls of the palace was a flat green space set aside for exercise and sport. Whenever I could find the time I sneaked away from the kitchens to watch the bowmen at practice. Some were passing good, though none was excellent; and for the most part their shooting with small bows and indifferent arrows was a mockery of marksmanship.

But one afternoon there came to the butts a thin, greying scrag of a man carrying a bow as tall as himself. I went up to him and remarked pertly:

"Sir, that's a fine bow."

"The best bow in England," he answered, smiling. "It is Spanish yew."

"Sir, may I shoot with it—just three arrows?"

He looked at me in astonishment. And in a moment he gave a laugh so disbelieving that a spurt of anger ran through me.

"Let me shoot and I'll shoot a better mark than anyone in Winchester!" I cried.

"Better than *anyone,* my urchin?"

"That I will!" said I, very sure that I could do so.

He narrowed his eyes at that, intense blue eyes, deep set in the thin pale face.

"Let me see you at thirty paces."

I set up a wand at thirty paces. He handed me the bow and watched me shrewdly as I balanced it between my hands. Oh, it was a beautiful bow, strong and pliant, yet so light that I could imagine it as part of my own body, an extension of my arms and hands.

"Three arrows, boy." I let them fly: one, two, three. They all but split the wand in twain, and I saw the man's eyebrows arch up, and heard the surprised click of his tongue.

"Three more at sixty," he said.

I set the wand at sixty paces. My three arrows all hit the mark, two dead centre and one to the edge, within a hair's breadth of missing altogether.

"A badly shaped arrow," said I. "Or badly fletched."

He smiled at that. "I'll speak to the villain of an armourer! Now set the mark at a hundred and try six arrows. Here's a score you can choose from."

I set a wand at a hundred paces and carefully chose six arrows. The man watched me with a sort of detached curiosity, as if he were more interested in me than in my skill as an archer. A small crowd of onlookers had gathered around us, and in my silly way I was determined to impress, to show off, to draw from this gentleman the admission that I was a very fine bowman indeed. I could feel a gentle wind blowing from the south and before I took my stand I tested its strength with a wetted finger.

Then I let my six arrows go; and when I had two in the air at the same time, I heard the man give a little whistle of surprise, and somebody, I know not who, cried, "Bravo!" Both these arrows missed. Of the others, two struck fair, one a little leftwards of centre; the last clipped the top of the wand, and reared high, and fell sadly, like a maimed bird.

"Good shooting, boy," the man said when I was done.

"Did I not say?" I answered boastfully.

"You said you would shoot a better mark than anyone in Winchester."

"Three and a near miss out of six at a hundred paces," I said. "Who can better that?"

He took the bow from me, and tested the wind as I had done. He chose six arrows, and took his stand. There was an air now almost of indifference in his manner. The arrows flew: one, two, three; a pause, then four, five, six. Every single arrow hit the mark.

Now, it is fair shooting if you hit a wand at a hundred paces with one arrow out of six. To hit with three arrows out of six is good, *very* good. To hit six times with six successive arrows is a miracle.

I stared my unbelief; and, remembering my loud talk and silly boasts, I felt the blood rush to my face, and I turned shyly away. The man took my shoulder.

"Wait! You have used my bow and abused at least one of my arrows. Don't I get a word of thanks?"

"I—I thank you, sir."

"You don't know me, boy?"

"No, sir."

He said lightly, to some behind him: "He doesn't know me, such is my fame!" And then to me: "I am Walter Tirel, Lord of Poix."

The name meant nothing to me. But now that he had told me, I could recognise nobility in the proud lines of his face, in his slender white hands, and in the quality of his tunic and leather shoes.

I muttered in confusion: "Your pardon, lord."

"What is your work, boy?"

"I work in the kitchens, lord."

"A scullion, by God!" he laughed. "Well, the King could make better use of you, my urchin! But you are not the best bowman in England—nor even the best in Winchester, are you?"

"I shall never best you," said I. He laughed again, well pleased. Then I asked: "May I go, lord? The cooks will beat me if I'm late in the kitchens."

"Oh, go," he said, "go!" But as I turned from him he called me back. "Here, take the bow! I'll get another as good! Let it be a prize for your shooting."

"For—for me, lord?" I cried in delight.

"Yes, for you, my urchin! Take some arrows, too—and come to the butts and practise often. You'll be the best in Winchester yet!"

At his words all my old cocksureness surged back into me, and I gratefully accepted the bow and half a dozen arrows (which he permitted me to choose) before hurrying away to my duties in the kitchens. But I never returned to the butts, for even then I realized that my ability with a bow was likely to attract too much attention there, and start up too many questions.

And apart from this, I was shortly to be overwhelmed by events that brought me to the edge of ultimate disaster.

11 An Unexpected Meeting

THE DAY started badly. Sleeping head to toe in a stuffy little alcove off the great kitchen, three of us young scullions overslept and were roused at cockcrow by a cook kicking us and calling us ill names. It seemed that the Steward had decided overnight that the rushes in several of the rooms were sour and must be changed; and so, after we had swallowed a quick breakfast, we marched into the palace and raked up the rushes, and carried them in armfuls to a spot outside the walls, and there made a splendid bonfire.

Though the rushes stank, we liked this labour. It was a change from the steam and the heat of the kitchens, in which you never got a glimpse of the sun; and you could always make pretence of being busy about the bonfire, when, indeed, you were simply lazing and larking behind the smoke screen.

It must have been near mid-day when we were finished. Then we were each given a sickle, and sent down in a wagon through the East Gate and across the bridge to a stretch of the river where the reed mace grows in a green swaying forest, so tall that it sometimes rises above a grown man's head.

This was better even than the bonfire. You could pretend to be lost amongst the reeds, and when your name was called you could lie low and answer nothing. Or you could pretend that you were drunk with the heavy scent of meadowsweet, or drowsy with the touch of poisonous henbane, both of which also grow abundant there. Our overseer was a lazy, good-natured old man, and after we had filled his wagon three or four times, he decided that he must rest, and so made himself comfortable on a layer of reeds in the wagon, and fell asleep.

We stripped off our clothes and went swimming. The water was warm under the hot sun and flowed over our naked bodies like a balm. My two companions were for splashing and games in the water; but I was possessed now with a sort of melancholy; and so I left them, and dressed again, and wandered away up the river bank.

Perhaps some secret instinct was reminding me that all our fun and laughter was for me only a make-believe; that I was in Winchester for a serious purpose; and that I must pursue that purpose with all the strength and determination that was in me.

Presently I found myself on the wide slope of St Giles's Hill, where every autumn is held the Great Fair, and which overlooks the bridge, the East Gate, and the nunnery of St Mary's. As I stood, watching moodily, a girl came through a narrow doorway in the city wall. She humped a basket to the river's edge, and there unloading it, started to beat a white sheet on a stone in the water.

It was Patrice.

My heart lightened as I hurried down the hill, cupping my hands round my mouth and calling her name. She looked up and knew me. I threw off my tunic and plunged into the river, and swam across to her.

Since leaving her with the goodwife, I had spoken briefly with her two or three times. Now, as she put down her linen, and faced me with bare arms and her fists doubled on her hips, I saw the healthy glow of her cheeks and felt sure she had plumped out a little.

"Is everything well?" I said as I came up. Then I saw that she was in a dark, dark mood.

She asked abruptly: "When will you take me from here?"

"Presently, Patrice."

"When's presently?"

"I don't know. Is anything wrong?"

"I don't want to stay here any longer. You must take me away."

"Doesn't the goodwife treat you kindly?"

"She—she's all right."

"Does she beat you?"

"No."

"Then what are you complaining about?"

"I'm not complaining. When will you take me away?"

"Where can I take you?" I cried impatiently.

"But you said . . ."

"I said that when my business is finished, I'll take you away. So I will, Patrice, I swear!"

"What is your business?"

"I can't say."

"Why can't you?"

"I—I am pledged to secrecy."

"Why is it such a secret?"

"I can't tell you."

"Well, when will it be finished?"

"Soon, I expect. Then I'll take you away and we'll go home together."

"Will it be tomorrow?"

"No, not tomorrow."

"The day after tomorrow?"

"I don't know when. What's wrong with you? Is it the old woman—what's her name?"

"Nell."

"Yes, Nell. Is she what's wrong?"

"I don't like her, Alan."

"Nor do I. But she hasn't harmed you?"

"No. But I don't want to stay here."

"You must stay till I'm ready. You must!"

"When will you be ready?"

"I don't know, I don't know!"

We were on the verge of another bitter quarrel. But at that moment a bearded face appeared over the wall a little distance away.

The man called sharply: "Give over your gossipping, girl! Get to your work!"

Patrice swung round, pale with sudden anger.

"How dare you shout at me!"

"Don't answer back, damn you! Get to your work!"

"Damn you, too!" she yelled.

The man bobbed down. "Who is he?" I asked.

"It's Asser," she cried. "Who does he think he is, I'd like to know! Does he take me for a serf?"

I seized her by the arms so roughly that she caught up her breath.

"A serf," I snarled. "Yes, that's what you are, Patrice! A serf, a washer-girl! It's as much as our lives are worth to put on your fine airs here! You're a serf, a serf! Don't you forget it!"

Then I left her and plunged into the river and swam back to the far side. For it was in my mind that Asser was a servant of the King, and I had no wish that he should report me to the cooks, or worse still, to the Steward, for laziness or neglect of my duties. I was glad to rejoin my two companions (both of whom I found sound asleep), and we busily set about cutting more reeds.

It was late in the afternoon before we returned to the palace with our last wagonload. There, after a meal, I was ordered back to my old chore of pot-scouring in the kitchen.

At this season the great oak-beamed dining-hall was used only once or twice a week when the King held a full table; for the most part Rufus preferred to dine in his private rooms with a few of his special companions. His guests and courtiers likewise dined privately, and the servants who had been allocated to them thronged the kitchens throughout the day, ordering food and drink and carrying it back to their masters.

Amongst these waiters was a scrawny youth with big yellow teeth, named Osbern. I heard by chance that he was attendant to Count Ralf, and at once I set about cultivating him in the hope of learning something of the Count's plans. Osbern was an empty-headed, boastful fellow, and he talked freely under the influence of a red raw wine which I was able to obtain from a boy who worked with the Vintner. He loved to gossip, to bask, as it were, in the greatness of his masters; but there was in him an evasiveness which made him chary of expressing a personal opinion. He dealt more with rumours than with fact, he seldom looked you in the eye, and you could never be sure that anything he said was true.

"Very handsome is milord Ralf," he told me. "Ah, a noble gentleman and a great soldier, too—he is, he is!"

"Does he see the King often, Osbern?"

"Ah, he do, he do! And they say . . ."

"What do they say?"

"He's going, they say."

"Going where?"

"Abroad, they say."

"Where abroad?"

"Well—they say France or Flanders."

"What's he going for?"

"What's he going for? Ah, lots would like to know the answer to that, wouldn't they?"

"Could it be to recruit an army of mercenaries?"

"Could be, could be, my lad."

"But he'd need a lot of gold for that, wouldn't he?"

"Ah, he would."

"Has the King given him gold, Osbern?"

Osbern winked and nodded sagely.

"The King loves him, I reckon. And you know what they say—why, they say those the King loves don't lack for anything, do they?"

I had learned something, but not very much. And then, just as I had decided without forethought to seek work in the royal kitchens, so now I impulsively resolved to seek out Count Ralf and to offer him my service in some capacity or other—as page, or under-writer, or valet-de-chambre, it mattered little what. For if I could get close to him, I would certainly learn much about him. I would keep my ears well pricked, I would listen by night and day, I would listen at doors and windows. Then perhaps I would hear of his plans from his own lips, and so know them for a certainty.

It was not until sunset, and curfew had sounded from the Minister, that I was free of my kitchen duties. Count Ralf's chamber lay in a part of the palace which I had never visited, but I had questioned Osbern artfully and I felt certain now that I could find my way there.

As soon as I could get away from the kitchens, I went down through the long underground passage running west, then up a stairway, along another passage, and at the end, a turn to the right. It was all as I had visualised it. I cannot recall that I was in the least daunted at the prospect of coming face to face with one who, with the Red King, I regarded as the chief of my enemies. Man as he was, old as he was, I felt confident that

I could match him for wits, for he would know nothing about me, he would suspect nothing.

As I made my way up those steep and narrow stairs, I rehearsed to myself what I should say to him: I would flatter him and call him a great general, and tell him my father had died fighting for his cause in the fells, and that it was my earnest prayer that I should serve him as a page.

Yes, that would do very nicely.

I reached the upper passage, and turned to the right. Through an open doorway at the far end I heard voices. I went forward without hesitation. The room was lit feebly by a rushlight; two men stood within, much engrossed in talk. A short man had his back to me; the other was tall and elegant, with a white spike of a nose and a mass of silvery hair, and I rightly took him to be Count Ralf.

"My lord," I said. He did not hear me. He did not see me. "My lord," I said again. And now he looked over his companion's shoulder, and frowned.

"Who are you?" he asked irritably. "What do you want?"

"I am Alan, lord," I said.

At that his companion turned. He stared at me; I stared at him in a shock of disbelief.

It was Father Benedict.

Pursuit 12

I SAW ONLY the face of Father Benedict, the deep furrows, the sadness, the fixity of his dark eyes, as it might have been a disembodied face in a dream. The rushlight spread its tender glow over his features, all else about him was lost in shadow. My mind did not move. I was conscious only of the immensity of surprise that now possessed me.

"Why, Alan," said he.

I did not speak.

But I was beginning to remember.

I remembered the last night we had spent together after my interview with Earl Bueth; how I had said I was going to Scotland to carry an order for swords to a Scotch armourer, and how I felt in my bones that he did not believe me. And I remembered he had told me that he had been summoned to the Abbey at Penrith for a month, there to pay penance, and certainly I believed him.

But now he was here, in the palace of the Red King, in the Red King's capital, far, far from his penance in Penrith. Oh, it was hard to believe he was not a phantom, some figure of my fancy, even though he stood before me, even though he had spoken my name with the gentle intonation that I knew so well. He spoke it again.

"Alan . . ."

I was silent.

Then, as I stared, his lips turned in a tiny hooked smile. He averted his eyes as if wishful not to face me, and in their depths there passed a look of deceit and shame and slyness, such as I had never seen in him before. This expression came and went quick as thought, quick as the beat of a linnet's wing. Then again he looked at me foursquare, his mouth set straight, his eyes sad with the old, deep sadness. But it was too late. Already I knew: I knew as surely as if he had shrieked a confession to me, that he was a traitor.

"Alan, what are you doing here?"

I did not answer. He reached out a hand. I knew it for the hand of death and swerved away.

And now the room behind him shaped and hardened from the shadows. I saw again a bed, a table, stools; the slit of a window holding a splinter of pale evening light; Count Ralf, angry and bewildered, his hair framing the long face like a halo.

"Come, Alan," Father Benedict said.

Suddenly panic seized me.

I screamed: "Traitor, traitor, traitor!" And I fled.

I could hear the two men pursuing me. I could hear them shouting: "Stop him, stop the boy!" from Father Benedict; "Guard, Guard!" from Count Ralf in a shrill voice like a woman's. At the turn of the passage I looked back. Father Benedict was in front, the silver mane of Count Ralf seemed to be suspended over his left shoulder. Their feet pounded the passage like a distant drum.

I leapt down the stairs. At the bottom, a serving man, about to ascend, paused, snarling: "Eh, what's this, what's this?" His eyes swung upward. "Eh, what mischief is it now?" The shouts grew louder, nearer. I ran on.

A frenzy of fear possessed me. I could think only of escape. For to be caught was death, a death terrible and unthinkable! If Count Ralf had not divined my purpose, he would drag the truth out of me with gouges and hot irons! And when Father Benedict denounced me, as he surely would, as an enemy and a spy, they would torture me in slower measure, with weights and wheel and knives, they would flay the living flesh from my bones.

Even as I ran, the imagined agony wracked me. I had lost all sense of direction and fled I knew not where. I fled from passage to room, from room to stairs and cellar, from cellar to passage. I fled past shouting men and grimacing serving women. It was as if the whole palace was roused in uproar; I had a fearful sense of being trapped there as a bird is trapped in the fowler's net. Between the stone walls every sound was magnified, every footfall, every cry, rose up to mock at me. I came to a door which I thought would lead me to the ramparts. But even as I reached it, it was flung wide, and a man lunged at me, calling: "He's here! I've got him!"

I slipped beneath his arms and ran on.

In the narrow passages, on the winding stairs, I was more agile than a grown man. In my anguish I thought: I must keep running! God's mercy, I'll keep running and they'll not catch me! It was a wild thought, a wild prayer. For now many had joined the pursuit, they were like hounds hunting a poor exhausted beast. And even though you know a terrible death awaits you when they close for the kill, you cannot run for ever; terror gives strength but not unlimited strength. Your pace falters, your head swims, you stagger on blinded with tears until at length your tortured heart cries—Halt!

I came to an empty room, a fine, wide room, and there I crawled beneath an arras and lay there defeated, waiting for them to find me. Presently a number of men came in, three or four, perhaps; I could not see them but I heard them cursing and moving the furniture. One of them actually lifted the arras which concealed me, but because of the deep shadows, he did not see me inert upon the floor. I wondered then, I wonder now, that he never heard the pounding of my heart.

The men departed. I lay still, listening, listening. The silence was heavy about me, more terrifying even than the tumult which had followed me. For the tumult told me where my pursuers were, the silence betrayed nothing. But I knew they would still be searching for me. They would search every corner, every alcove, every chest and cupboard, until they found me.

I could not stay here. I must sneak away, trusting that somehow I might reach a doorway that would lead me to the ramparts or the yard. Ah, if I could have but one breath of sweet night air, one glimpse of a twinkling star! I clasped my hands and in my heart I spake a prayer, seeking God's mercy and the guidance of Gabriel. The sweat jerked coldly down my cheeks, my heart quietened, I felt easier.

At last I rose. I would not leave the room by the way I had entered; some might be waiting and watching in the passage. I tiptoed through a doorway into another big room where was a couch, and the walls were hung with tapestries, and even in the greyness of the dying day, the furniture glistened finely. I stood uncertainly, peering about for another exit from the room. Seeing none, I was about to turn back, when a movement in the corner held me rigid.

In a moment a man emerged from a concealed privy, pulling up his hose as he moved and grunting with the effort. His head was bent as he concerned himself with his dress, a big head of fair thick hair cropped at the neck in the French style; and he came out lumberingly to within an arm's length of me before he saw me.

He gasped and stopped short. Then, with a wonderful agility for so gross a man, he stepped back and swung to one side, positioning himself between me and the doorway.

"How—how came you here?" When I did not speak, the blood rose swiftly from his neck to his temples, and in a great voice, he bellowed: "Ah—ah—answer me!"

But I did not answer him.

Deep inside me old memories were stirring. Five summers had rolled away; I had returned to the great camp in the great field by the lake of Windermere; and I saw again the flash of the executioner's sword as it clove my brother's throat; and I heard again Edward's dying shriek; and I watched his life blood spilling on to the grass. And through it all a pot-bellied tyrant looked on in silence, his chin supported on the flat of his hand.

Oh, I knew him! I knew him beyond all doubt, beyond all possibility of error; for that image of him, in all its detail, was deep graven in my memory. He stood before me now, stammering, "Ah—ah—answer, boy!" He was the Bastard's son, Rufus the Red King.

"You are the King," I whispered.

"By—by the face of Luke I am the King! And those who tres—trespass on the King's privacy do suff—do suffer f-for it, boy! How—how come you here?"

The big face was so close to mine that I could see the saliva bubbling on his lips as he struggled with his words. Truly, I think that in that moment all hope was dead in me. I was delivered to the Arch-tyrant, I had reached the end! Then again I thought of Edward, and in the flood of misery and despair which swept over me, I cried aloud: "Oh, Edward, Edward!"

"Edward? Is—is it your name?"

"My brother's name," I said.

As I spoke, my left hand chanced to press on the horn handle of my knife, which was thrust into the belt beneath my tunic. I took a step back and slipped my right hand into the opening of my tunic.

Rufus said: "Your br-brother? Where—where is he? Here in the palace? Is he—is he? Tell me!"

"He is dead, King."

"Dead? Dead? What is it to me that your brother is dead?"

"You killed him, bloody murderer!" I screamed, and I pulled out my knife and lunged at the King's breast.

I saw the King's ruddy face thrust close to mine, his lips drawn back, spittle on his chin. He gripped my wrist, the knife fell. He gripped my throat. His strength was monstrous, it was as if great pincers held me. I remember his great thick forearm covered with fine golden hair. I remember how he lifted me, and thrust me hard against a wall, and held me there helpless, my feet a-swinging. And how it seemed that iron bands tightened round my chest, and bells crashed in my head; and that my tongue swelled monstrously and was forced out through my teeth.

And that, for a little while, is all I remember.

When I recovered I was lying on the floor. Rufus stood above me in a stammering frenzy. Behind him, in a crescent, were ranged a score of others. I saw Father Benedict and Count Ralf far back, as if wishful not to know me now. I saw Sir Walter Tirel at the King's elbow, turning my knife in his slender hands. And in a moment, Sir Walter spoke.

"Why, the young bowman! And treason truly! But where from, sire?"

"God knows!" cried Rufus. "God knows! He tells of a brother, Edward."

"He tells as he's been told. He's but a boy, and boys don't usually traffic in treason. Who sent him?"

"By the face of Luke, he'll tell us! T-t-to-tomorrow he'll

confess all, I promise, and he'll suffer as all traitors s-suffer! Take him away, fetter him! Let a priest shrive him! I'll have him fl-flayed and his guts fed to the crows! T-take him—take him!"

Two men dragged me to my feet, and bundled me into the passage, thence through a doorway, and so on to the rampart of the palace wall, all the time beating me about the head and face.

Even though I knew what was happening, I knew it only vaguely, as if I were living in a dream. But as we came into the darkness and the cool night air, it was as if a light suddenly blazed in the cavern of my mind. I became alert, instantly aware of the peril in which I stood. I realised that my guards were hurrying me towards a stairway, that we would descend the stairway, down, down, to a dungeon where they would fetter me.

And once the fetters were on, I would be lost.

As they dragged me along the rampart, I felt the beat of rain on my bruised face, I glimpsed tiny bouncing fountains of rain on the puddled flagstones. One of my guards slipped slightly in the wet, and it came to me, with the force of a physical blow, that both men were shod with leather, whereas I was barefooted, for I had long since discarded my own broken shoes.

And it was then that a voice deep, deep within me shouted: "Now, Alan, now, now, now—before it is too late!"

I suddenly threw my weight against the man grasping my right arm. He grunted and fell away into the darkness. I butted my head into the face of him on my left, and brought my knee up hard into his belly. He groaned and was gone. I ran to the edge of the wall: one, two, three paces, as I clearly recall. I heaved myself over, and for a moment I hung there, clinging by my fingertips, seeing nothing in the darkness, but knowing of the long drop to the fosse below.

Then I let myself go. As I struck the ground, a sickening pain ran through my right foot.

I lay a long time in a stupor. At last I crawled and stumbled along the base of the wall, and all the while the rain lashed me harder and still harder. And this was God's rough mercy on me; for, looking back, I believe it was the rain that saved my life. It thrashed and soaked and alerted me, so that I could not rest; it forced me, miserable, shivering, and wracked with pain as I was, to seek a safer shelter than the palace fosse where, with daylight, I must have been discovered.

I never found shelter from the rain. But when daylight came the storm had passed, and I was hiding in the long grasses on St Giles's Hill.

In Hiding 13

IN THE days that followed my misery and my loneliness alike were great. My foot turned blue and swelled to a monstrous size, and I had no herbs or balms to cure it. At nights I would creep secretly to the river and there bathe it and bind it with damp grasses. But for many days the pain was fierce; there were times when I thought that life was ebbing from me, and hope itself was dead.

But hope is never dead whilst you are aware of night and day, of sun and wind, of thirst and hunger. I had all the river to drink from, but for a week or more I did not dare to go there except at nights. On those swelling hillsides there is precious little shelter from a scorching sun, and during the day I was plagued by maddening thirst. Pain and hunger weakened me, for I did not eat so much as a crumb of bread for five whole days. And then, such is the goodness of my guardian Gabriel, I scraped friendship with two sailors from a deep-water ship anchored downstream from the bridge. I played the simpleton with these good men; and they, out of pity, gave me bread and meat and fish. In return (I confess it to my shame) I stole from one of them a slender, horn-handled dagger.

The bruising passed from my foot, the pain eased. But my fear was such that I would lie trembling at the sound of a distant voice, and sometimes I would take refuge on the other hill of Winchester named St Catherine's. It lies near a mile south of St Giles's Hill, and on its crest there are the fosse and vallum of an ancient fort, built long ago by savage men before the coming of the Romans. You could lie safe and snug in the deep fosse, sheltered from the blazing sun and the prying eyes of men.

Yet my favoured spot was St Giles's Hill. For though reapers came there most days to cut and turn the grasses, and so added greatly to my risk of discovery, I found comfort in the sight of the great city beneath me.

I could look down on streets and the bridge, on the mill and water meadows, on the dark spire of St Mary's Abbey, the nunnery which King Alfred's queen had founded; I saw little Fearless on her long tether; I saw Patrice and goodwife Mercy Asser busy with their laundering; and my heart seemed to turn in my breast at the sight of Patrice kneeling, beating her linen on a stone. She was my friend, we had travelled far and endured hard things together.

One night I swam across the river, and beneath the layer of reeds at the bottom of the old boat I uncovered the bow and arrows Sir Walter Tirel had given to me. Next day I shot a couple of rabbits which I carried to my sailor friends. They questioned me hard about the rabbits, which had obviously been killed by arrows; and I played the simpleton, saying they had been given to me by an old woman for some errands I had done for her. But my tale did not convince them, I realised I had aroused their suspicions, and after that day I never returned to them.

The days passed. I grew stronger, and, I think, bolder; and it was borne in on me that the time had come for me to return home and report to my lord. I wished I had some definite news regarding the plans of Count Ralf Meschin to carry to him; but I had not, and it seemed that I had now learned all that I was likely to learn in Winchester. I realised, too, that every day—nay, every hour—I remained here, added to my dangers, and that if I was discovered I should suffer unbearable torture and be put to shameful death.

Patrice, of course, would return with me, and I would have to think of some way of getting a message to her. Nor did I mean to leave Fearless behind if I could help it, so that I should have to devise a means of getting the little mare out of the city.

I was pondering these problems one morning from the summit of St Catherine's when I saw a lean and youthful figure ambling across the bridge. It was Osbern. I saw him put out a small boat, and row a little way upstream, where he stopped, and threw out a fishing line. I watched him for several minutes. I did not like Osbern, I did not trust him; but now, impulsively, I resolved to speak with him. I descended the hill, avoiding the reapers, and taking off my tunic, plunged straight into the river.

He was engrossed with his line and did not see me until I reached my hands to the side of his boat. Then his eyes widened and he puffed out his cheeks and slowly deflated them, hissing through his big yellow teeth. I levered myself up on one elbow and clambered into the boat.

I said: "I want your help, Osbern."

"Treason!" he whispered. "Treason so it was! Holy Saints, I wouldn't be in your shoes!"

"I can look after myself," I said.

"They'll tie you to horses, and whip 'em, pull out your legs from their sockets! They'll fill you with water till your belly bursts!"

"They won't catch me."

"Ah, they will, they will!" He baited his hook clumsily with a pellet of bread. His hands were shaking. He muttered: "There's a reward out, they say."

"For me?"

"Ah. Fifty marks if you're taken alive, they say."

"What! When did you hear this?"

"Yesterday. Yesterday morning."

"Well, they won't catch me."

"They will, I reckon."

"I say they won't!" I cried.

This was my brazen talk. But in truth, I was as frightened now of Osbern as he was of me. Fifty marks! That was a fortune, enough to tempt any righteous man, any honest man! And Osbern wasn't righteous, he wasn't honest. I watched him through my lashes, as he smiled abstractedly to himself, looking across the river, a shimmering flame in the morning sun. I felt sure he was thinking of fifty marks.

"You won't betray me, Osbern."

"No. . . . No, I won't."

"Because if you do, and if they catch me, I'll have a pretty tale to tell."

"Eh? . . . What tale do you mean?"

"I shall tell how you inspired me with your own hatred of the King, and gave me a knife, and showed me the way to his private rooms."

"But—but it isn't true!"

"They'll believe it, Osbern. They'll believe it because I'll swear to it and you'll confess to it. They'll put us under torture, and you'll confess to anything they want you to confess."

"No, no!" he moaned, rocking on his seat. "You wouldn't tell such lies!"

"It's what I'll tell them if you betray me."

His long face crumpled as if he were about to cry.

"Damn you! Why do you plague me? Go away! Go!"

"I'll go when you've told me things I want to know."

"I won't tell you anything!"

"Why aren't you with your lord this morning, Osbern?"

He paused before he answered: "I—I'm at liberty."

"Where's Count Ralf?"

"He's gone from Winchester."

"When did he go?"

"Yesterday morning. Now go away! Leave me alone!"

"Where has Count Ralf gone?"

He paused again, battling with his fear.

"If—if I tell you, will you leave me alone?"

"Yes. Where has Count Ralf gone?"

"To—to Flanders, they say."

"To raise an army? With money borrowed from the King?"

"Well—that's as they say."

"Is it true, Osbern—is it?"

"It's true," he breathed.

"How long will he be away?"

"I don't know, I don't know!"

"But you must have some idea. You've waited on the Count night and day. You've listened to his talk."

"Well—well, perhaps six months. He has hopes of being back by Candlemass, that's in February."

"With an army?"

"Yes." He placed his hand pleadingly on my arm. "Alan, you wouldn't tell those fearful lies about me, would you?"

"God knows what I would tell if I was caught, and they

were disembowelling me," said I. "I would try not to tell lies about you, or about anyone, I would try to keep my mouth tight closed and endure it unto death. But how can I promise? How can anyone promise? Best not to be caught."

"That's it, that's it," he nodded. "Go away, never come back."

"It's what I mean to do," I said.

His hand was still resting on my arm. I don't think he was aware of it. He was looking fixedly again across the river, as if his thoughts were far, far off. But, indeed, they were not; for in a moment he remarked:

"When you came to Winchester, there was a girl with you."

"You mean my sister," said I.

"Your sister, is it? Where is she?"

"Gone away."

"Gone where?"

"Never you mind," said I.

"Holy Saints, I mind!" he cried. "There's a reward for her, too. Thirty marks, they say. If they catch her, they'll make her talk, they'll make her tell things, won't they? Will she tell those lies about me, too?"

A coldness swept through me and seemed to touch the deep core of my heart. He was looking hard at me now, he must have seen the anguish in my eyes. I forced out a laugh. "Oh, but they won't catch her," I said.

"God help us if they do!" he answered quickly. "Now go away. I don't want to be seen talking with you. Go away, don't come back!"

I dropped over the side of the boat and started to swim. I felt his sullen, frightened eyes watching me all the way into the cover of the reeds on the distant bank.

14 In the Mist

I CLIMBED the steep hillside, but seeing some of the workers eyeing me curiously as they turned the hay, I sought the refuge of St Catherine's. There, throughout the long hot afternoon, I lay concealed in the fosse of the old fort.

There was a sort of numbness in me. I tried to bring some order and good sense to my thoughts; but always I was haunted by the image of Patrice, I would hear her voice begging me to take her from the goodwife's house; and I remembered how I had refused her, and a bitter anguish seized me and the tears fell from my eyes.

Yet what other course had been open to me? A spy is a solitary creature, of necessity he works alone. I could not have had Patrice with me in the kitchens, or in any other place, whilst my real work in Winchester was still undone.

As I lay in the deep fosse, a skylark rose above the hill. His song throbbed sweetly on the air long after I had lost him in the blue, and I had a strange fancy of myself winging high and far, with a glorious freedom, and leaving my miseries behind me. Perhaps I drowsed momentarily, perhaps I dreamed. I cannot say. I only know that a measure of calmness came to my distracted mind. And again I tried to reason things out.

It had never occurred to me that anything I had done, or had failed to do, would endanger Patrice. Indeed, I believed I had done well to leave her in the care of goodwife Mercy Asser. But now I thought of the reward of thirty marks for Patrice, a great fortune for a peasant crone like old Nell, and my heart went cold within me.

I thought of Osbern. And suddenly it struck me that he, being employed at the palace, would be amongst the first to hear of the rewards that were offered for our arrest. Even within the city walls news travelled slowly, for few could read (not even the Red King knew his letters) and even if our descriptions had been called by a Cryer, most citizens would know nothing of it until it was reported to them by their neighbours. Therefore the chances were that at present only a handful of courtiers and palace servants were aware of the rewards offered for our arrest.

Nevertheless, Patrice—living and labouring inside the city, within an arrow's flight of the palace walls—was in fearful danger. By morning she might have been seen, recognised, taken. I dared not attempt to get her away before nightfall, for if I was arrested, that would be the end for both of us. Equally, I must get her away, and Fearless, too, before the night was done. Tomorrow might be too late.

Thus I reasoned after many hours.

In my reckoning I made no allowance for Osbern. How could I? I had no means of telling whether he would keep mum, or whether the great bait of fifty marks would tempt him to inform against us. I did not trust the scamp; nevertheless, I was inclined to think he would probably hold his tongue, lest, if arrested, I should involve him in a treason plot.

I watched the sun go down in pink splendour beyond the West Gate. Then I crept down from St Catherine's and made my way once again to the slopes of St Giles's. The reapers had gone, all was quiet there. As I waited in the twilight, a sheeps-wool mist rose from the river, and spread, thickening, into the water meadows, poking long fingers at the city walls, the roofs, the spires.

I descended the hill, breathing a prayer of gratitude for the shelter of the mist. Half way down I stopped. Beneath me, the mist was cut off cleanly, almost as if with a knife, at the top of the city wall, so that there was a clear space to be seen dimly beyond the wall. I heard a voice far off, a woman's voice, calling or shouting. Then I saw Patrice carrying a linen basket towards the town. She moved slowly, the basket was heavy laden. I saw good wife Mercy close behind her, carrying a stick. It was the goodwife's voice I heard, though I know not what she said, she was too far off. I seemed to glimpse another figure a distance behind them, a shadow in the shadows, but I could not be sure. The mist rose in a white mantle, and all was blotted out.

One thought was foremost in my mind as I sped down the hill: that Patrice must not go near the palace, above all she must not enter it, for she might never come out again. I plunged into the river and ran to the door in the wall. It was bolted, locked. I ran on until I came to a place where roughened stonework made it easy to scale the wall. I dropped down on the far side into well-nigh blinding mist, and it was sheer luck that almost at once I recognised the outline of the goodwife's house looming through the whiteness.

Within the hut the fire was burning low and the four half-naked children were gathered by it in a forlorn little group. I yelled at them, demanding to know where their mother and Patrice had gone. They only stared. I yelled again, and one of the girls started to cry with a shrill, breathless sobbing, such as only a child in mortal fear can make.

I left them and ran towards the town, sure of my bearings now. I came to the bridge, turned into Chepe Street, and started up the long slope. Buildings loomed dark and shapeless on each side of me. Far off a dog howled. Then all was silent save the slip-slap of my bare feet upon the ground. I had a feeling of unreality, as if I had entered a place that existed only in my imagining, a town of phantoms.

Then, from far up the street ahead of me, there came a scream.

It was a fearful sound, seeming to echo agonisingly in the mist. But I had no time to be frightened. I knew that somehow I was involved with that scream, that I must press forward and discover what had happened. I felt so sure of this that I shouted: "I am coming! I am coming!" And my own voice seemed to echo about me, too, and to deride me as I ran.

I came first to the linen basket upended and its contents spread in the roadway. Three steps further on, the goodwife lay so still that at first I thought she was dead. There was blood, blood everywhere, gushing from a wound in her right shoulder. A knife, the thin blade dark with blood, lay beside her. I made a pad from a linen sheet and tied it to her shoulder, and so staunched her bleeding.

She lay passive until I put my lips to her ear and said distinctly: "Where is my sister? Where is Patrice?"

She stirred. She looked well enough, as if she were sleeping. I did not think she would die. "Where is Patrice?" I said again. "Where is she?" Slowly she opened her eyes. I was bending close over her and I saw the swift awakening of her mind.

I saw recognition and fear start in her eyes. She started to scream again. I clamped a hand roughly over her mouth. "Where is Patrice—where, where?" She understood, I could tell from her face that she understood. Yet, as I took my hand away, she screamed again: "Help! Murder! Help, help!"

Then a man seized me by the neck. "What's this? What's happened, you villain? What's going on?"

I did not even look at him. I wriggled from his grasp and fled.

Throughout that night I roamed the city, seeking Patrice. I combed the streets not once but half a dozen times; I searched the narrow alleyways and courts; I went into the churches and into the churchyards; I pried, so I believe, into every midden heap, into every hole and every corner of the city.

Sometimes I heard footsteps and voices echoing in the mist. I fancied I was being followed, and I hid awhile in a courtyard or in a doorway until I thought the danger had passed, and then I hastened on. How far I walked, or where exactly I walked, in that interminable night, I cannot tell, for mercifully I do not remember.

Only this I know, that I could not find Patrice.

With the first uncertain light of day and the crowing of the cocks, a breeze sprang up from the hills in the east, driving the mist before it. I crept down to the bridge. Now all hope for Patrice was dead, I felt sure she had been arrested. For myself I was beyond caring. I tumbled into the old boat in the cornfield against the river.

An inexpressible weariness of mind and body possessed me, the pain of great loneliness was with me. I closed my eyes and lay still, and in my heart I prayed for God's relief in my travail. When I opened my eyes golden sunlight was flooding from a cloudless sky. And, looking down on me over the stern of the boat, was the crone, old Nell.

I don't think I felt alarm or surprise. It had happened before, it was like a senseless recurring dream, me lying prone in the boat, and her little dark face and her dark flashing eyes peering over the gunwale.

Nell said: "You shouldn't sleep. You'll be catched if you sleep."

"I shan't sleep," I said.

"Fifty marks for you," she said.

"I know."

"Thirty for her, for Patrice. I heard Mercy say. Thirty marks the King would pay, Mercy said. She were taking her there."

I sat up quickly.

"Taking Patrice to the palace? Mercy was doing that?"

"Ah, she were, she were selling her, beating her with a stick!"

I cried: "Where's Patrice?"

"She aren't your sister."

"All right, she's not my sister. Where is she?"

"In sanctuary, that's where!"

"What sanctuary?"

"The abbey, St Mary's—the nun-minster. 'Tis God's ground, holy ground. They durstn't touch her there."

"You mean—she's *inside* the abbey?"

"She is, she is!"

I clutched her wrists and pulled her so close that her face was almost touching mine.

"Is she hurt? Wounded?"

"Nay!"

"How do you know she's inside the abbey?"

"I took her there," Nell said.

I let her words sink in.

I was kneeling now, as she was. The sunlight fell full upon the old worn face, the impish eyes. Something impelled me to turn her hands—how thin, how claw-like, how bony, yet how strangely strong! There were stains like rust upon the palms, stains that ran high over her wrists, and into the loose skin between her spindle fingers. She was watching me closely and she must have seen that I understood the nature of those stains, for she yelled, her eyes flashing with quick anger:

"She'd abeen sold for thirty—sold like Jesus was for thirty! That Mercy—she's a sly one, she's wicked, wicked! But they shan't harm Patrice now, the King shan't have her! 'Tis holy ground where she be!"

I scrambled from the boat.

"Hush now, Nell, or you'll have everyone know what you've done. They'd hang you for it!"

"But you won't tell, you won't tell!" she wailed.

"Mind you don't tell that you've talked with me, or it'll be bad for both of us," said I.

And I ran off through the sunlight towards the abbey.

Escape 15

I SOUNDED the bell at the gate. After an interval, an elderly nun in a wimple and black mantle opened the grille and looked out at me. I begged for admittance, saying I had come to fetch my sister who had been brought there overnight for shelter. "Wait!" the nun answered simply, and closed the grille.

I stood with my back to the roadway and the bright, revealing sunlight shining down on me. I died a dozen deaths as I waited, knowing that any passerby might recognise and seize me. A waggoner passed, making for the bridge, then a horseman, then two or three more on foot. I heard them greet one another, very close their voices sounded. A pigeon rose from a nearby tree with a loud clapping of his wings. Another wagoner came down the slope and stopped. I dared not look at him. It was hard not to turn and run, madness though that would have been. I screwed up my courage fiercely and moved a step nearer the gate, and stood motionless, feeling sick with fear. An eternity passed before I heard the sliding of a bolt.

The gate opened a little way, I stepped within.

"Mother Abbess will speak with you," the old nun said, closing the gate. "Come."

I followed her across a courtyard where the warm flags struck comfort to my feet. Low buildings stood on three sides of the yard, and the Sisters were busy inside them, some preparing food, some laundering, others sweeping and cleaning, their mantles tucked up and their feet bare, like peasant women. We passed by the chapel and the great dark tower, and came to a cloistered walk. At the far end a doorway stood open. The nun, without a word, motioned me into the cell beyond, then went away, closing the door behind me.

After the brightness of the yard, I stood for a few moments narrowing my eyes at the shadows of that small room. It was a cool, dim cell; the floor was bare, cold stone; the only piece of furniture was a low wooden couch. On the bed sat a tiny, plump woman of about fifty; her hands clasped in her lap. Framed in her wimple she had the face of a man, and not a handsome man at that: cheeks puffed up and covered with fine veins, the mouth wide and set in a firm line, fine hairs on her chin.

She looked at me for a long minute without speaking. Then said she, very quietly:

"I am Mother Abbess. What is your errand, my son?"

I told her that I had come for Patrice, my sister. When she did not reply, I added anxiously: "The old woman, Nell, said she brought her here last night. Is she not here, Mother?"

"The child is with us, my son."

"God bless you for your charity, good Mother. Now let me take her."

"Do you know why the child was brought to us?"

"I know only what Nell told me."

"Do you know that the woman called Mercy was with this child last night, and that Mercy was grievously wounded with a dagger?"

"No!—I mean, yes. . . . Yes, I know it, Mother."

She was silent, watching me closely with solemn grey eyes.

I said: "It was not I who wounded Mercy."

Still she did not speak. I said: "I am sure it was not Patrice."

"How are you sure, my son?"

"Because—because Patrice wouldn't do a thing like that! . . . And—and when old Nell came to me, I saw—I saw her hands. . . ."

"What of her hands, my son?"

"Never mind! Patrice did not attack goodwife Mercy. You must believe me, good Mother!"

"Do you know that the King has offered a reward for the arrest of this child?"

O God, O Gabriel, help me now! I prayed. God help Patrice, don't let her be taken, God! Don't let them torture her, don't let them put her to death, O God!

"I know of the reward, Mother Abbess," I said.

"Why do you wish to take the child from us?"

"I—I want to take her away . . . far away."

"Where far away?"

"To the north, where I belong."

"Do you know the King has offered a reward for *your* arrest, my son?"

O Gabriel, don't desert me now! I prayed. O God, you have watched and guarded me, you have kept me safe thus far, God! Don't betray me to my enemies!

"I have done no wrong, Mother Abbess!" I said.

"Did you not attack the King?"

"I . . . I . . ."

"Spare yourself, my son. This child, Patrice—is she indeed your sister?"

I hesitated long. Then I answered: "No, Mother."

"Tell me your tale. Tell me who are you and who is this girl you call Patrice, and what you are doing here. And tell me the truth, my son."

Whilst I was talking she did not stir, she did not once interrupt me. But as she sat with her plump little hands folded, her tranquil eyes searching into me, I became subtly aware of her personality, of her pure inward strength and dedication to the things of God. I told her all my history except the important fact which I was under solemn promise not to reveal, that I had been sent to Winchester to spy, saying that I came there as fortune took me, which was a sort of half truth. I told her my name and that I hailed from the land of the Lakes; and how the Red King years ago had slain my brother and my father with the utmost cruelty, and I came close to tears in the telling. I told her who Patrice was, and how I had met her in the Fens, and how her father and his followers had been slaughtered, and what we had since endured together.

She was silent for a space when I had done.

Then said she: "There is a demon of hate in you, my son."

"Yes, Mother," said I. "The demon is always there when I think of my brother Edward."

"Your brother Edward," she said earnestly. "Is *he* the reason why you attacked the King?"

"What other reason could there be?"

"My son, there are many who hate the King. There would be few to grieve for him if he were dead. He has wrought great cruelties and evils, some say he worships Satan, certain he has robbed Mother Church to enrich himself. And some men declare openly that one so steeped in sin as Rufus is not fit to rule, and it would be well for England if he were dead, and another reigned in his place. Tell me truthfully, did any such men speak with you? Or hire you to attack the King?"

"Mother, I know nothing of these matters—I swear it by Holy Cross! And I swear also that it was not I who wounded goodwife Mercy."

"I know, my son."

"Nor was it Patrice!"

"That also is true."

"So you believe me?"

"I, too, saw blood on the old woman's hands. More, I heard from her own lips that she had done it to save the child from being taken to the King."

"Nell did that? The old woman did that?" I felt a burden lifted from me. "She did it from charity, Mother—she did it for Patrice! You will not betray her?"

"What she did is between herself and God, my son."

"And the goodwife? I tried to help her, I staunched her wound. For all Mercy's wickedness, I'd not have her die."

"She was brought into the abbey for our care. I think she will not die. I have sent two Sisters to her house for the children's sake, and a message has gone to her man, Asser, who is at Malwood, making ready for the King's hunting. There is nothing more we can do."

"God reward you for it, Mother. But—but there is Patrice."

"Yes," she answered gravely. "Yes, there is the child."

She took up a clapper bell from the floor and sounded it; and when the old nun appeared she ordered that Patrice should be called.

After a long interval Patrice appeared. For a moment she stood in the doorway, darkly outlined against the bright sunlight of the cloister, a forlorn, frightened figure. She did not see me standing against the inner wall, and as she walked slowly into the cell, prodded forward by the nun, I could tell that she had been crying bitterly. My heart moved for her, she seemed so frightened, so alone. Slowly she raised her eyes and saw me, and an expression in which gladness and hope and fear were strangely mingled settled on her face.

Mother Abbess asked: "Do you know this youth?"

"Yes, Mother."

"He wishes to take you from us."

"I'll go, Mother!"

"But listen! If you stay here, you will always be safe within these walls, always. Do you understand, child?"

"But—but Alan?"

"He could not stay here. That is impossible."

"I will go with Alan," Patrice said.

I stepped forward. "Then now she can come?"

"I have not said so," Mother Abbess said.

"But, Mother, *she* has said that she wants . . ."

"I have heard what she says. I have heard what you have said. But, my son, my duty is neither to you nor to the child. It is to God."

I said, aghast: "Do you refuse to let her come with me?"

Mother Abbess gave a little shake of her head.

"There is another demon in your heart, my son, the demon of arrogance. You should learn of your saints the lesson of humility. And consider, if I let the child go, what dangers you both face. If you are recognised and taken to the King, expect no pity there, for pity is unknown to him. And how shall I answer to God for her death and yours?"

"But what is to be done?" I cried in desperation.

"Let us go to the chapel and seek God's guidance," Mother Abbess said.

I was wracked with a misery more bitter than before, and Patrice's face was white and crumpled, as if she wept within herself with a grief too deep for tears. Within the small stone chapel there were soft shadows and quiet and the scent of herbs in the still, warm air. A slender shaft of sunlight from a high window fell slanting across the nave, two candles burnt un-flickering at the altar.

Mother Abbess motioned us to the altar steps and bade us

kneel. "Pray for grace and guidance, my children." She knelt behind us, near to the door, and I heard her softly reciting the *Credo* and the *Pater Noster*. I knelt with my hands clasped and my eyes half closed, possessed with fearful bitterness. God knows, I had need of grace and guidance, but I could not pray. It was as if I had emptied myself of prayers, or had forgotten how to pray. I watched tiny wisps floating silver in the sunlight, vanishing into the shadows. Ah, if we could vanish from this chapel, which had become our prison, as swiftly and as certainly as that!

The chapel now was silent. I became aware that Patrice was not praying either. She had lowered her hands and had moved on her knees a little way along the step towards me.

She whispered: "Don't leave me alone, Alan."

"No," I said.

"Keep me with you."

"Yes," I said.

"What can we do?"

"I don't know," I said.

We might have been inside a tomb, it was so quiet there. Time passed; then I heard the soft drop of the latch of the chapel door. I waited. The silence was solid. And Patrice, looking furtively over her shoulder, whispered:

"She's gone."

I rose, rubbing at my knees. Yes, Mother Abbess had left us. And I saw on the flagstones by the door a dark bundle which I felt sure had not been there before. It was a pile of clothing, neatly folded. I went to it and picked up the garments, uncomprehending. Then suddenly my heart leapt with overwhelming joy.

There were two nun's dresses, two wimples, two girdles each carrying a crucifix, and a purse of six silver pennies. Patrice stared, a little fearfully.

"What are these things? What are they for?"

"For us to wear."

Still she did not understand.

"I don't want to be a nun! I won't be!"

"We are going from here," I said. "We are going home, Patrice."

I bade her put on the smaller of the dresses. It was too long, but she hitched up a length and held it firm under the girdle. I put the wimple on her head and arranged the folds carefully round her little dark face, and it was a transformation so complete that I think her father would never have known her. I put on the other dress and had her arrange the wimple, and she could not forbear a smile, though she was weeping a little, too. We practised a way of walking up and down the chapel and we did not forget to pause a minute at the altar and speak our inadequate little prayer of gratitude.

Then said I, "Shall we go?" and when she eagerly answered, "Yes," we stepped into the sunlight of the yard.

Nuns at work there did not heed us. There was no guardian at the gate. I drew back the bolt and we passed into the street.

Scarcely an hour later you might have seen two nuns passing through the city's East Gate, one walking and leading a horse on which the other was riding. You would have said probably that they were two novices dedicated to some errand of charity, or setting forth upon a pilgrimage. You would never have dreamed that under her mantle one of the nuns carried a slender, horn-handled dagger, or that beneath the horse's blanket were hidden a dozen arrows and the best long bow in England.

The Second Day of August 16

It was much in my mind that as soon as our escape was known a hunt would be made for us, and that, since our objective was the north, the search would be concentrated on roads leading north and north-east. I decided, therefore, to turn south and then west on leaving Winchester, heading for the old city of Salisbury, and to make thence for the Lakes along the western edge of England.

It struck me, too, that we could not sustain our disguise for any length of time, and would have to discard it fairly soon. Anyone travelling with us must have wondered at the depth and huskiness of my voice, or the mannish length of my stride. As for Patrice, however well she looked at a distance, the impish childishness of her face was plain enough for anyone to see close at hand.

I bade her keep her hands clasped and her eyes cast down, which she did well enough for a few miles; but as soon as she felt our immediate danger was over, she burst into laughter and started singing. I could not find it in my heart to blame her, but I was more alert to our hazards than she, and in a temper I swore at her, and told her to shut her mouth and keep her eyes down.

We followed the road south to the old port of Bitterne for several miles, turning west before we had a sight of the sea. We rested that first night on the edge of a heathland where grew tall pines and birches, and great spiked bushes of furze. At dusk I managed to shoot a hare which I skinned and cooked, kindling a fire from pine needles and cones with sparks struck from a roadside flint.

In the morning we set off again, still in our nuns' garments. And this day, as many clerks and historians of England have recorded, was Thursday, the second of August, in the Year of Our Lord, 1100.

Before long, Patrice, in her teasing mood, started singing and laughing, and even made a pretence of blessing with her upraised hand a man riding by on a donkey. And of course, we squabbled again, and in the end I gave her a sharp slap across the face, and she came at me angrily with her fists, and I had to throw her down. After that, we travelled on in silence; and as I tramped along the dusty road, mile after weary mile, my thoughts turned back upon myself, back into the past. I recalled the lakes and the fells, Tom and the sheep. I recalled my brother Edward, and a hardness came into my throat.

At mid-day we rested for two or three hours and finished off the remains of the hare. I had not ridden Fearless so far because I thought that two nuns riding a single horse was a sight that might attract unwelcome notice. However, my feet were sore; and so I mounted, and with Patrice behind me, we continued at a steady pace. The road had become rough and narrow and there was little traffic on it.

Towards evening a man on foot lifted his hand respectfully as he passed us. My head was cast down, but glimpsing him from the tail of my eye, I felt there was something familiar about his tall, bearded figure. I felt Patrice's arm tighten on my waist as she whispered:

"Asser!"

"Are you sure?"

"Of course I'm sure! Do you think he knew us?"

He was striding on. "No," said I. "He didn't know us. Don't look back."

A few minutes later, the blast of a hunting horn floated through the trees to our left. And I recalled what Mother Abbess had told me, that Asser was at Malwood to prepare for the King's hunting. Clearly then, Asser was now on his way to Winchester, to give comfort to goodwife Mercy, and we were close to Malwood, and all this wide heathland was the King's New Forest.

I thought of Rufus, Edward's bloody murderer, with his gross bulging belly and his heart of stone. I thought of him hunting out there, serenely riding the forest glades; and I thought how good, how just, how wonderful it would be if the King himself were hunted, if Death stalked him unsuspected as he stalked the unsuspecting deer.

Why not?

I had the means with me, the bow, the arrows. Why not, indeed? I seemed to see Edward again, his hands severed, his throat gashed wide, his blood spilling, I seemed to hear his voice lifted in that last agonised cry—a cry for revenge, for justice!

I thought: I will do it—Edward, I will do it!

I drew Fearless off the road, into a pretty spinney of beech and oak through which a streamlet trickled.

Patrice asked: "Why are we stopping here?"

"Supper," said I.

"But we have nothing to eat!"

"I am going to kill something."

"Let's go on," Patrice said. "I'm sure I heard hunters close by."

"They won't harm you. Stay here, don't wander. I may be away some time."

She sensed the hardness of my mood and said no more. I slipped off the nun's dress and wimple, took up the bow and half a dozen arrows, and left her.

I walked over the road, over a ride of thick, springy turf, and into a woodland. Now I had forgotten Patrice, I was obsessed with thoughts of Edward, of Rufus. In a little while I heard again the soft repeated bleat of the hunting horn. I reached the edge of the woodland and waited.

I had not long to wait.

On a distant slope a bunch of beaters appeared. They came forward, stopped, then spread themselves into a wide half moon over the full width of the slope. The light was splendidly clear out in the open; though they were far off, I could see fine details of the men's appearance, their hair, the varied colour of their tunics, I could hear the murmur of their voices. Each man carried a stick, except one in the centre who seemed to be the leader, and he had a yellow baldric over one shoulder, to which was attached a horn. At his heels loped four great dark hounds. The men took up their positions, then stopped again, awaiting a signal. It came at last, a horn blast from the woods at the foot of the slope. Slowly they moved forward.

I knew nothing of the ways of huntsmen. But it was clear that the beaters, who now were thrashing their way slowly through grass and bracken, were intent on driving the deer into or through the wood, and that somewhere down there the King would be waiting. Therefore I had but to move before the beaters (as if I were a deer) and sooner or later I would come close to the King. The thick woodland afforded me all the cover I needed. It was all too simple.

I turned back into my own little strip of woodland and hastened down the slope. At the bottom, where the trees gave out, lay a broad, marshy ride. Any open space, such as this, was a hazard, and though I could see nobody about, I went down on my hands and knees and crawled into the woodland beyond. And it was as well I did so, for I had scarcely reached the trees on the far side, when a forester on horseback or a huntsman, I know not which, appeared at the top of the ride, and came trotting past me. I rose and waited until I saw the first of the beaters appear at the top of the ride, then I turned into the deep wood.

This ancient place is called the Stricknage Wood, as all the world now knows, although I did not know it at the time. It is a wood of great beauty and abiding peace. You can stand beneath the ancient oaks (for it is mostly oaks) with the soft green light all about you, and high above, the branches sway and murmur, tipped buttercup bright with the sun; and in the slender patches of blue above the trees, swallows flash and skim, a kestrel hovers.

I now moved forward with the greatest caution, passing from tree to tree and pausing every few paces to watch and listen. But I was not in the least afraid. A sort of drunkenness was in me, filling me with an ecstasy of power and hatred; I had not the slightest doubt that before another hour had passed, I would have settled my account, and Edward's, with the tyrant Rufus. I must have gone far into the wood (I took no account of time or distance) when I came upon another broad glade or ride. Then I heard voices and the rattle of harness.

I dropped to one knee behind a towering elm. I could see a

long way leftwards into the glade. The sun was behind the horsemen and almost directly in my eyes, so that for a few seconds I could not distinguish them. Then the foremost rider turned to his companion: it was Rufus, sitting like a great toad in his saddle, the reins loose in his left hand, his fair, windblown hair standing like a brilliant crown on his head. Beside him rode Sir Walter Tirel, his eyes thoughtfully cast down. The third rider was a groom.

They dismounted a short distance away. The groom handed bow and arrows first to the King, then to Sir Walter, and led the three horses back down the glade. Sir Walter pointed and said something, but I could not catch the words. He stepped into the cover of the trees, as if he intended to take his stand at that point. The King spake nothing but ambled on alone. He passed some fifty or sixty paces from me, and I could hear him twanging the string of his bow with his thumb as he walked, testing the tension.

I could have shot him then, no doubt. But he was sideways to me and moving all the time and I wanted to be certain of a kill. At length he halted by a solitary tree in the middle of the ride. I can see the exact shape of that tree as I pen these words; it was a magnificent oak of great age, very wide in its lower parts, and tapering to an almost flat top, like the bastion of a castle. I can see the flickering light and shade of its fronds, the long blue shadow it cast across the sward. The King turned so that he was almost facing me and raised his hand, signifying that he was ready. The signal was somehow relayed to the beaters, for shortly I heard the bleat of the horn, the yelping of hounds, the sound of men thrashing through undergrowth and bracken.

For some minutes nothing happened. Then, from my side of the wood, a stag trotted forward uneasily, a splendid beast in the full vigour of life with enormous, widespreading antlers. It trotted towards Rufus, then stopped, its great head uplifted, full of suspicion, perhaps scenting him. And Rufus, fearing to lose such a beast as this, quickly loosed an arrow.

But the distance was great. The arrow took the stag in the shoulder, and it turned and went off down the glade like a hurricane. It sped straight into the setting sun; and Rufus, taking two or three steps from his stand, stood watching it intently, shielding his eyes against the glare of the sun with his right hand.

Now was my time, now my opportunity.

He was standing quite still, no more than fifty paces from me. And he was positioned almost foursquare to me, so that his great broad chest made the easiest of marks. I took an arrow and nocked it on my bow, a thrill of excitement running through me. I fought it down, I mastered it—you cannot aim fair with shaking hands or sweat in your eyes! With the crotch of my thumb I could feel the arrow snugly nocked on the bowstring. I did not look at it, I was watching Rufus.

And there he stood, absolutely still, his hand shading his eyes.

I was about to raise my bow when the unimaginable thing happened. Even now, after this lapse of time, I find it hard to believe. And yet I know it happened in just the way I describe, for I was close to Rufus, and my eyes were full upon him, and never left him.

And it happened with fearful swiftness, swifter by far than any words can tell. An arrow struck him in the chest. His right hand dropped from his eyes and clutched at the arrow which was protruding from his tunic. He fell on his face and lay still. I heard the snap of the arrow shaft as he struck the ground.

And that was all. He gave no cry, he made no sound whatever.

I was so stupified that I looked down to make sure that I had not unknowingly loosed my arrow. But no, the arrow was still nocked on the string. And suddenly I was frightened, terribly frightened. I was caught up in mysteries beyond my understanding; I had the notion that God had been watching me, watching me for days past; that God was jealous of me; and that now, having miraculously forestalled me in the killing of Rufus, God would punish me for my arrogance in his own terrible fashion.

Everywhere was tumult and confusion; men bawling and shouting, hounds baying, horns sounding. A sweat of fear poured from me as I waited for God to strike me down as he had struck down Rufus. And when death did not immediately come, I crept behind the trunk of the elm tree, then swung myself up and stretched full length on a broad low limb. There, as I watched the small excited crowd gathered round the King's body, a measure of sanity returned to me.

God had not struck me down as in my terror I thought he must. And now I pondered it, I could not believe that he had struck down Rufus either. I had not followed the fatal arrow in its flight, but I had seen it protruding from the King's breast and I could easily assess its line of flight. It was not God who had shot that arrow but a man. I felt certain, too, that it was no accident. There was no stag near the King, there was no reason why anyone should shoot an arrow in the King's direction—except to kill the King.

And I recalled the words of Mother Abbess, that there were many who hated Rufus, and some said he was not fit to rule, and it would be well for England if another ruled in his place.

Except for myself there was nobody within a hundred and twenty paces of Rufus when he fell. They say a man's heart is no bigger than a clenched fist; thus, whoever killed Rufus hit a mark as small as a clenched fist at a distance of a hundred and twenty paces.

I believed there was only one man in England who could shoot as wonderfully as that, and the arrow's line of flight confirmed my conclusion. The Lord of Poix, Sir Walter Tirel, had killed the King.

I had not observed Sir Walter in the excited throng about the King's body. Yet he must have seen the King fall as clearly as I had. What had happened to him? I fancied him in headlong flight (this fancy, as things turned out, was true); I saw him making for the coast, perhaps for Bitterne, there to ship for France and to take refuge in the lands of Poix.

For a long time I lay motionless in the elm above the glade. I saw the men and hounds depart, I heard horses galloping off through the trees. I waited for some to return to take up the King's body. But none came. The sun dipped and the darkening tide of night flowed almost imperceptibly through the quiet forest. Presently I glimpsed a star winking through the branches overhead and a young moon threw its wan light into the glade.

Still I waited, and still none came.

Beneath the oak tree lay the shapeless bundle that had been England's King. At length I climbed down from my branch and, bow in hand, I crept across to him. Some unfriendly foot had turned him, so that now he lay on his back with his arms outflung. I knelt and looked into his face, ruddy even in death. Not a handsome face, I thought, nor yet a face of evil. I touched him, his forehead, his thick fair hair. My heart stirred strangely. For the living Rufus I had known an intensity of hatred. For Rufus dead I felt only overwhelming pity.

I crossed his hands on his breast and hastened away through the wood. When at last I rejoined Patrice she clung to me piteously, and sobbed: "Oh, I've been so frightened—so many shouting men! Where have you been all this time? What is wrong?"

"The King has been murdered," I said.

"Murdered—oh! . . . Alan, did you . . . ?"

"I did not," said I. "But who's going to believe that? If they catch us here we shan't live to see another day."

Then quickly we gathered up our things, and I mounted Fearless and pulled Patrice up behind me. And so we fled northwards through the night.

Home Again 17

On a soft grey day towards the end of the second week of August, we passed the waters of Windermere and ascended the northwards pass beyond Great Gable. We had journeyed fast and without incident: from Malmesbury, where we abandoned our disguise, to the Welsh borders, then north again to Lancaster and Ambleside. Poor little Fearless was as skinny as a beanpole; she had carried us bravely and without complaint, and now, on this last homeward stage, we marched beside her and let her strike her own pace. We were sweating and footsore and dark with dust, and when at last we came to a beck, we stripped naked and swam and splashed in the cool waters; and Fearless stood knee-deep with us and whinnied as if she could not understand a magic that turned us from brown to white.

It was late in the afternoon when we descended by the Grey Knotts. The sun had broken through a sky of shreds and tatters, and far below us lay Falconsdale, the fells swelling up green and blue from the silver thread of the lakes; and all as still as if nobody had ever trodden there before us. Patrice looked down with her hands clasped and her eyes full of wonder, and Fearless scraped the hard ground uncertainly, for neither of them had ever known a land like this. As for myself, I came near to tears, and I breathed a secret prayer of thanks to Gabriel for his watchfulness and to God for our deliverance.

We continued on our way without haste. Towards evening we came down through heather and bracken; and there beneath us were fifty or sixty sheep—our sheep, mine and Tom's—cropping the coarse fell grass. And there, too, loping down a path was Tom himself, his long arms clasped at his back, and his hair bunching like a white hood on his shoulders.

I cupped my hands round my mouth and gave him a shout, and he stopped, looking towards us with his hand shading his eyes. We pushed on quickly and shortly came up with him.

"Why, Alan," said he; and that was all he spake. I put my hands on his shoulders; and at the contact I felt his unhappiness run through me.

"Aren't you glad to see me, Tom?"

"You went off without a word, Alan," said he.

"Oh, Tom, I couldn't help it! I was—ordered."

"Ordered? Well, none told me that. I took it hard, boy. Where've you been?"

"Winchester."

He pursed his lips. "Then it's good you're back." And he turned to Patrice. "Who's she?"

I told him her name. And she, with her brown eyes sparkling, stepped towards him and cried with passion: "I'm the daughter of Wilfrid, that's who I am, old man!"

It was a better answer than mine.

Tom regarded her for a moment or two with mild surprise. Then suddenly he seized her by the waist and lifted her high as he might have lifted a cornsheaf.

"That's a fine thing for a lass to be!" said he.

Shock and indignation showed in her dark little face. "Put me down, put me down, put me down!" He swung her down, then lifted her higher than before—for, despite his rheumatics, there was still great strength in those long arms of Tom's. And Patrice, helpless as he swung her up and swung her down, suddenly threw back her head and pealed with laughter, a shrill, joyous laugh such as I'd never heard from her before.

And Tom laughed, and I laughed, too; and to myself I thought I would not exchange the love of these two friends for all the gold in the Red King's Treasury.

We spent that night in our old hut beneath Birk Crags. And, of course, we talked far into the night—at least, Tom and I did. I showed him my bow, which he declared to be the finest he had ever seen, and I told him something of our adventures, particularly that part concerned with the Fens, though there was much that I was not yet at liberty to disclose even to him. I said that I must report to Earl Bueth on the morrow, and that if he, Tom, was willing, I would leave Patrice and Fearless in his care, for they were both worn with the long journey, and I would make my way to the Manor House on foot. He was agreeable to this, for he had taken a great liking to Patrice.

She was still sleeping when I set out in the morning. I went down the long slope, where every cobweb and every leaf and grassblade flashed gem-like in the dew, and the rooks complained loudly overhead, smelling a change of wind and weather, and the sheep looked at me, and looked away again, not bothering. I went down the old remembered ways, through the bracken and the grass, and I saw the bilberries ripening, and whorls of mist rising like smoke from the good earth, and the cloud shadows chasing over the fellside. I felt the beat of the west wind in my face, and saw the white cloud ribbons clinging to the peaks, and the dazzle of gold when a sunbeam touched the distant lakes. And when I came to the lakes, I dangled my feet as I had dangled them a thousand times before, and I found the rowing boat where I had always moored it amongst the reeds. As I rowed down the length of Ravensmere, listening to the creak of the oars, the tinkle of the water, the complaints of the water birds, I could believe that time had stood still here, that I was a small boy again, sneaking away on a secret fishing expedition, or on some archery practice, when I should have been at my lessons.

I left the boat at the landspit, and walked slowly down by Heronwater, passing kitchen, bakery, and armourer's shop; and the armourer, working at his anvil, called to me that he thought rain was blowing up, not realising I had ever been away. I said I thought so, too, and walked on to the Manor House, where men and women were busy at their chores, and none gave attention to me. It was always thus, you were taken for granted here, you had your own business to mind, and they minded theirs.

I went in, and as I came to the fire, one of the yellow hounds came forward and snuffled my hand. I knelt and fondled the dog, which he tolerated well enough, then I looked up over his great smooth head to the platform, where my lord sat in his chair.

He was talking with Father Benedict.

For a second or two I stood dumbfounded.

Not since that dreadful night in the Red King's palace had I seen Father Benedict and I had scarcely spared him a thought. Now here he was in his drab monkish gown, his hands clasped, smiling his wan little smile as he listened to what my lord was telling him. Oh, it was hard, so hard, to believe! And then a flame of anger swept through me, and I leapt at him, shrieking the one word that came to my tongue.

"Traitor! Traitor!"

He turned. You would have thought I had thrust a knife into his bowels. I knew he had forgotten me, or given me up for dead. "Alan!" he breathed. "Alan!" He ran his tongue over his lips. Expressions of shock, consternation, and fear moved swiftly across his face. He raised an arm—whether to greet me, or to strike me, or to ward me off, I cannot say.

I beat it down, screaming, "Traitor!" and I struck at him.

Then men seized me and threw me down, and presently forced me to my knees at the platform's edge. A dozen were gathered there now, and Father Benedict stood in the midst of them, his hands still clasped, his face turned from me. And on the platform, with his hounds beside him, sat Earl Bueth, small and strangely bent in his chair, and with a crooked smile at one corner of his white mouth that was not a smile at all, but something hideous and frightening.

"Stand, boy," said he. And when I stood: "Look at me, answer as I say! Where have you been these many weeks?"

I told him.

Then he asked: "What news have you of Ralf Meschin?"

I told him.

Then said he: "Why do you call Benedict a traitor?"

I told him. But even before I had finished Benedict, one foot on the edge of the platform, cried: "Lord, the boy wrongs me! Truly he is out of his senses! I was never in Winchester."

"Why should you be in Winchester?" Earl Bueth said. "What business could take you there?"

"None, lord! I was not there!"

My lord turned his green eyes full upon me. He seemed so small, so white, so misshapen.

"You hear, boy? He was not there! Now what say you?"

I took a deep breath, for I was trembling within. "He was there, lord. He did the things I say he did. He was as close with Count Ralf as two peas in a pod! And you may be sure he has betrayed our secrets to him. Why otherwise should he deny he was in Winchester?"

"Good Benedict," Earl Bueth said, "tell us where you went when you left here those many weeks ago."

"I went to Penrith, as I have said. I was at the abbey making penance."

"And when you came back, Benedict, you brought us news we had not heard before—that Rufus was slain and Henry ruled as King of England."

"True, lord."

"How did you learn of this?"

"A message was brought to the abbey."

"You would swear to this?"

"I swear to it, lord."

There was a long minute of silence. The old man's white face flushed red, the crook of his lips seemed to deepen. With an effort that set his whole body shaking violently, he raised himself in his chair, and in a voice that rang through the room, he shouted:

"You are forsworn, Benedict! You are a liar!"

"My lord . . ."

"Hear me! When you spoke of the death of Rufus and the crowning of Henry, I wondered that you knew these things before us, for we have our means of knowing. But this I thought, that if you were not in your cell at Penrith, if you were at Winchester, it would explain how you knew these things before us, and brought them to us pretending your friendship."

"I was at Penrith, lord. I was at the abbey!"

"So you tell me now, so you told me then. Yet I was not satisfied. So I sent Godfric to question the Abbot at Penrith. Is Godfric here?"

Godfric, tall, dark, his sullen mouth bulging, answered: "I am here. It is true, lord. I went to Penrith and questioned the Abbot. He knew nothing of the death of Rufus, or that Henry was King. He had received no message from Winchester."

"And what said he of Benedict?"

"He said that he had not seen Benedict at the abbey since last spring a twelvemonth."

"Thus you are proved a liar, Benedict," Earl Bueth said; and although he spoke quietly now, there was an edge of ice to his voice. "We have given you our love through many years, and now, because you see us old . . ."

"You totter at the grave's edge, old man!" Benedict cried in sudden angry defiance. "Soon you will be dead—and what then, what then? Milord Ralf will march hither, and slaughter without mercy, and lay everything to waste because of your stubbornness! I acted for the best, hoping Ralf could bring you to reason, for you will never prevail against his army."

"We will fight, we will win as we have won before," Earl Bueth said. "As for Ralf Meschin and his brother, we will grant them six feet of our land apiece to bury them, and that is all. And you, Benedict, who have betrayed us with lies and cheating, shall have your own little piece of earth beside them."

"Don't touch me!" Benedict shouted. "If you harm me, all the wrath of Mother Church shall fall on your shameless head!"

"Take him," Earl Bueth said. "Take him, let him pray this night. Tomorrow he shall hang."

He was led away, struggling and shouting. When I would have followed to the door, my lord motioned me to remain. So I sat on the edge of the platform, awaiting some further sign from him. He regarded me for a long time in silence, lost in his own unguessable thoughts.

Then said he: "Tell me again what befell you after you left us in the spring." And when I told him again, he said: "It was all well done, Alan. Now we must make ready to scatter the great new army that Ralf is gathering."

It comforted me to hear him speak my name. I smiled my thanks, and he beckoned me to sit beside him, which I did.

"It is true what Benedict said," he went on slowly. "I am old, Alan, I am very old." With a bony forefinger he traced the deep fold of flesh that crooked his lips. "See, this is a palsy that seized me soon after you had gone away. It flung me down, it struck me dumb, it hooked my mouth, it bound my arm and leg as if with chains. I am better now, though I cannot stir from my seat without help. It is a sign from God that I am in the winter of my age, that I shall not live much longer."

"Don't say it, lord!"

"It is idle not to say it, it is the truth." And as he spoke his eyes glittered bright with tears. "I do not grieve for myself," said he. "I shall not find it hard to die. But I grieve for my people. And truly, I grieve for Benedict. There is only one reward for such treachery as his, and he shall have it! But I cannot forget that once I loved him, and my grief for him is great. Leave me now, Alan."

On the Red Crags 18

PERHAPS I, too, should have grieved for Benedict. But somehow I could not. I had spent countless hours in his company, he had taught me much; but I think I never loved him as Earl Bueth loved him. To my young eyes he was so old, so wise, so clever, so sure of himself—qualities which set him far apart from me. In my heart I was always a little in fear of him. Besides, at that late hour of night when I parted from my lord there was in me such weariness that I could think only of finding some snug corner where I could sleep. I begged a mug of goat's milk from an old woman in the kitchen, then curled up in the rushes just inside the main door of the hall.

It seemed I had scarcely closed my eyes before I was roused by a bearded fellow shaking my shoulder. I remember how he thrust his face close to mine, and that his long nose gleamed faintly in the firelight, as he whispered:

"Benedict has gone."

"Gone where?"

"Escaped."

It took a moment for this to sink in; and even then it was not so important to me as sleep. I replied that I did not think he would get far in the darkness.

The man answered: "He must be taken. That is the order. There's no telling what further mischief he will do if he reaches the enemy."

I asked what he expected me to do.

"You can stir yourself and help to find him," the man retorted roughly. "You know the mountains and the passes better than we. Stir yourself, damn you!"

And with that he grabbed me by the neck of my tunic and jerked me to my feet.

Horses were waiting in the yard. There must have been a dozen in the party and Godfric was the leader. The night was black as pitch as we set out for High Fell and the Red Crags in the teeth of a westerly gale, making a smart pace, for Godfric knew this part of the track very well. I rode alongside the bearded man who bellowed the information that Benedict had taken a horse and had a three hours start of us, and was last seen skirting the northern edge of Haw Tarn.

In that howling wind conversation was impossible, for your words were killed on your lips as you uttered them or scattered over your shoulder. But I did not need to know more than what had been told me. If Benedict had passed beyond the Tarn, he was certainly heading for High Fell, and I wondered at his temerity in attempting that passage on such a night as this. I would have called it folly in any sort of darkness, but now, in the solid darkness that comes before the dawn, and in the teeth of wind and rain that scourged like a thousand whips—now, I say, it seemed a double madness. Of course, if he succeeded, he would save many hours and many miles; once over the heights, he would make the easy descent into Bardale, and so come to the coast where William Meschin had posted his strong garrisons.

We rode low on the necks of our steaming horses, and within a few minutes of starting we were soaked to the skin. You could tell from the pace of the horses that the ground was rising in a gradual slope, but the slope became steeper and steeper as we progressed. Shapes emerged mistily from the darkness as the dawn broke; a boulder, a bush, a tree. But it was grim dawn that disclosed a pall of grey cloud draping the fellside not far above our heads.

Suddenly a horse whinnied in the gloom and came towards us, and two of our number recognised it as the horse Benedict had taken. Obviously then, Benedict had dismounted hereabouts to make his way on foot. In fact, he had no choice, nor had we. Water was gushing down the track, tumbling stones and scree and eddying over the horses' fetlocks, and I, as the nimblest and most knowledgeable climber of the party, was thrust to the front.

Our pace now was very slow. Mighty fists of wind buffetted

us on face and shoulders, forced our breath back into our teeth, tossed a man's cap away like thistledown, flung another man flat on his back.

Then for a little the wind eased, the rain ceased. But you felt the lull was a deceit, that the mountain demons were but gathering strength to come at you more cruelly and fiercer than before. All about us slopes hissed and frothed and bubbled, great curving plumes of water spurted from the swollen becks. Then the cloud wrack seized us with great chill fingers; it was like creeping through a monstrous white wall. I could hear my companions groaning for breath behind me; and as we came up on to the exposed knife-edge of the western fell, where a frenzy of wind, sleet, and hail met us, they crept to the scant shelter of an uprearing rocky wall, and lay there, exhausted, helpless, beaten.

Only Godfric remained with me. There must have burned in him some bright valiant flame, for he was a dalesman, not a man of the mountains, and unused to such unrelieved cruelty as this. I scarcely saw him through the lashing hail and swirling mists that beset us, though he was hard behind me, but I could hear him moaning with his effort to keep up with me.

Now, the knife-edge ascends on your right hand to the Red Crags. the highest point of the fell; and this is the route into Bardale, though you would never think it. For Bardale lies far beneath you on your left, at the foot of Red Ghyll, a ravine which might have been made by a giant crashing his axe into the fellside with a single mighty blow.

Once, and once only, I had descended the ghyll when, on a fine, bright summer's day, I had rescued a cragfast ewe; and I had died a dozen deaths in doing it. It is a truly terrifying place, this ghyll, full of loose shale and scree, sheer and very dark in its depths, even in brightest daylight.

As we crawled slowly up to the ghyll I saw footprints leading to the broad lip. Fresh footprints, too, for they had not yet filled with water. I continued on up the knife edge, searching for footprints there. I saw none. I crept back and stared into the ghyll. Then I returned to Godfric and pulling him into the lee of a boulder, I put my lips against his ear and yelled:

"He has gone into the ghyll."

"Follow," his lips said.

I shook my head. "He will never come out."

"Never?" He did not understand. "Never?"

"It will kill him."

"Follow," he mouthed again; and he would have crawled into the ghyll had I not pulled him back.

"Fool! Here in the mountains I am the leader! Follow me!"

He hesitated a moment, then followed me back along the knife-edge.

In the next summer, on a bright morning, I again took the track to the Red Crags and the ghyll. I wanted to know what fate had befallen Benedict. I descended the ghyll; and a third of the way down I found him, a skeleton but still draped in shreds of his monkish gown, crouching on a narrow ledge.

I supposed that he had halted there exhausted, instinctively sheltering from the deluge of water and stones that fell about him. And I wondered what thoughts had moved in him as he crouched there, facing the westerly gale. Did he remember me with charity, the boy who had denounced him and so forced him to fly to this terrible and lonely place? And did he feel remorse for his treachery to the cause of free-born Englishmen?

There was nothing of pain or distress in his attitude, and it pleased me to think that death had come to him mercifully. I could not bury him, but I gathered many stones and laboriously built a cairn about him; and I knelt and said a prayer for him, as he himself had taught me.

I like to think of him resting quietly there until the great Last Summons.

The Plan 19

WE WERE kept busy making ready for the attack which we knew must come with the spring. There was much to do and little time to do it in; for we could not hope to drill and train properly, or raise new fortifications, in the depths of our northern winter.

Early in September, the Falcon summoned his Council, and though the many meetings were held behind closed doors, we soon learnt what had been resolved. I have told how our homeland was under pressure, by Ralf Meschin in the east, and in the west by his brother William, who had foraged down the coast as far as Ravenglass. At all costs we had to safeguard Falconsdale, the heart of our land; for if that was lost, all was lost; and we had to decide from what direction the spring attack would come.

There were three or four secret routes to Falconsdale, and it was possible, nay probable, that Benedict had betrayed them all. Only one thing seemed certain: with a new army at his back, Count Ralf would attack in great force, determined to crush us once and for ever.

It was a grim enough outlook. But I think none of us despaired, or even thought about defeat. For one thing, we had a leader whose long life had been dedicated to warfare against the Bastard and his brood, and who had never lost a battle. And besides, those of us who knew our country could reasonably anticipate Ralf's strategy. It was unlikely that he would attack from the west, where the mountain terrain is particularly hazardous for strangers; or from the south, where there is a wide area of almost impassable bogland beneath the Gable. No, he would almost certainly launch his attack from the east, for he had long held control of the old road to Carlisle through

Keswick, and he could move his forces along it swiftly and in comparative safety.

Lord Bueth, then, looked east.

From the Carlisle road a wide and easily followed track curls round the north end of Derwentwater and climbs through Belldale to the height called the Snab, where it bends leftward, still climbing, then opens into four tracks which drop sharply into narrow valleys.

Follow the first track on your right and in three or four hours it will bring you in sight of Ravensmere and Heronwater, and so to the entrance of Falconsdale. The next track to the left brings you into Longdale, a valley well named, for it takes you more than an hour to march from one end to the other. You are surrounded on three sides by steep slopes and towering crags, and there is no way out of the valley except by retracing your steps, or by climbing the narrow and precipitous path straight ahead over Hagfell, and only a fellsman familiar with its hazards would attempt that.

The other two tracks lead into valleys which yield good pasture and nothing else, and the tracks leading out of them soon bend back to the east.

Earl Bueth now ordered that the path to Falconsdale should be obliterated. It was an immense labour for hundreds of men over many weeks. Starting at the Snab, the track was lifted stone by stone, and every stone was carried up to the surrounding heights. Trees and bushes were uprooted, and where the track had been, turf was laid and bushes replanted. Then a small, tireless army of old men, women, and children, marched up and down the track into Longdale, some of them leading cattle. For the plan was to give the impression that the Longdale track was the time-worn secret route to Falconsdale; and thus to entice the entire enemy army into Longdale, and there to destroy it.

After I had laboured on the track for a week or so I was recruited into a specially formed company of archers. We had many good bowmen in the fells but only a few were expert with the long bow. In our company there were seventy men, all marksmen, and we practised archery several hours each day, sometimes at butts in the valley, sometimes on horseback (which is very difficult), sometimes on the lakes, shooting from moving boats at marks set up along the shore. We practised also with the sword and pike, we drilled, we wrestled, we exercised over the steep hillsides to strengthen our leg muscles. In hard weather, when drill and archery practice was impossible, we shaped new bows and arrows, so that by Christmas every man had two good yew bows and several hundred arrows in reserve.

Meanwhile, our armourers worked day and night on swords, daggers, axes, pikes, and shields, carpenters were building boats, the mill wheels clattered ceaselessly, flour and grain were carted to an immense new granary in the depths of the valley. If Ralf Meschin planned ultimately to starve us out, he would himself be dead of disappointment and old age long before any one of our number so much as felt the slightest pangs of hunger.

It was inevitable that in these autumn months I saw nothing of Tom or Patrice. I thought of them often, for truly my heart was with them under the pearl-white skies of the fells. I was a boy of the mountains, there lay my true home; I had often described them to Patrice, telling her how we would settle down with Tom and the sheep, not thinking I should be summoned away so soon and for so long. And I remembered how she had questioned me hard, and her eyes had shone, and I knew this was what she wanted.

Once I sent a message by a man going up by Birk Crags, saying I was well and busy, and would be with them as soon as ever I could. But whether they ever received the message I did not know. I heard nothing from them; up there on the fellside they lived in a different world, and I wondered how much they knew of all the preparations for war.

But at last there came a day when I found the opportunity to visit them. I climbed up to the Crags with a splendid west wind in my face that set my blood a-tingle; and there was a sharpness in it, too, and I knew that the hard weather could not be far off. Tom received me soberly. He had heard of our activities, and I am sure he suffered a secret grief that he was too old now for military service. He begged me to remind Earl Bueth that he could still draw a good bow, and I promised to do so if the opportunity came. But I knew that he could best serve our cause in caring for the sheep.

"You'll be bringing the sheep down to the dales soon, Tom," said I.

He nodded. "There's the smell of snow in the air. But it'll hold off for a few days yet, I reckon. We'll make a start getting the sheep down in the morning."

"Wish I could stay to lend a hand," I said.

"Patrice is a right good shepherd's boy," he answered genially. "She's not afeared to climb where my old legs won't carry me. She's a good cook, too, better cook'n you, Alan."

Patrice had had little to say to me, and whilst I was chatting with Tom, she sat apart, with what I thought was a shyness in her. But it was not really shyness. Presently I went across to where she was sitting cross-legged, preparing some meat for the pot. She looked up at me sulkily, her lips pouting.

"Why won't you stay?"

"I have other tasks, Patrice."

"What other tasks?"

"Training, getting ready for a battle."

"You think more of your silly bow and arrows than you do of me or Tom!" she cried.

"That isn't true."

"It *is* true, otherwise you'd stay! You're mean, you're mean!"

The unfairness of it stung me. "You know I can't stay," I said sharply. "I'm sure Tom's told you why."

"And what did *you* tell me? Didn't you say we'd live together, you and me and Tom, and we'd look atter the sheep, and that was all you wanted? Didn't you say that?"

"Well, I spoke too soon. I spoke without thinking. There's going to be a great battle, Patrice, and I . . ."

She flung down her knife and the haunch of meat she was carving and jumped up to face me.

"You don't have to fight in any battle!"

"You're a fool, Patrice!" I shouted.

She came at me with her fists, as she had done on another occasion, screaming: "You're mean, you're mean! You tell me lies and I hate you, bastard boy!"

I took her by the arms and threw her down and left her snivelling in the grass. Tom, who had heard us squabbling, came across to me.

"That wasn't well done, Alan."

"Little vixen!" I said.

"She has a fondness for you, boy."

"A strange way of showing it," I said.

"Maybe," said Tom. "But it's true, natheless. Now go back, and pick her up, and make it up with her."

I hesitated, for she had hurt me. But there was a compulsion in Tom's eyes I could not withstand, and so, after a moment I went across to her. She must have heard the rustle of my feet in the grass, for she jumped up before I reached her, and put her arms about my neck, crying piteously: "Don't go, Alan! Oh, don't go, don't go!"

I gave her what comfort I could, and promised to visit them again at the very first opportunity. But in my heart I was utterly miserable, for I knew there was a possibility that I might never see either of them again. It was Tom, good wise old Tom, who said that I must leave at once if I was to reach my camp before nightfall; and that having left them, I should march resolutely on, and not look back.

So I left them, and did not look back.

The Battle of Longdale 20

EARLY IN April we learned that Ralf Meschin's new army of Flemings and Frenchmen had landed on the western coast at Providence Bay.

It was said to be an army which put to shame the ruffian soldiery of William Meschin, who had joined forces with it. There were two companies of cavalry, and the several regiments of infantry, comprising axemen, pikemen, swordsmen, and archers, were wonderfully equipped. So, at least, rumour said. But we knew that rumour could lie and we were sure of nothing except that the attack would come in the dry months of May, June, or July.

Earl Bueth sent out scouts and spies, some of whom, alas, never returned. Those that did largely confirmed what we had heard: that the enemy force of between six and seven thousand men outnumbered us by almost three to one. The discrepancy was great and in open terrain no doubt they would have crushed us. But we did not intend to fight in the plains but in the hills, and we had an inspiration which those accursed foreigners lacked. We were fighting for our homeland. We never despaired.

Count Ralf marched his men eastward along the old road where River Cocker runs. Where would they halt? Where would they turn and strike? We sent out patrols, and it was my fortune to be posted to the slopes above Lindale, a point where the enemy might possibly swing south and strike for Heronwater. From the heights we watched their scouts testing the ground; the dale was narrow and due to the heavy winter snows, the bog lay deep and widespread. And so they marched on to the east, and when the danger of an assault through Lindale had quite passed, we were recalled to our base camp.

We knew now that the attack must come through Belldale.

We continued to drill and exercise as before. And we hated it, thinking we had had enough drill to last the rest of our lives. What we longed for now was battle, the real thing, to get it over and done with for better or for worse. There was rumour and counter rumour. The attack had started, it had failed, it had never started at all, it had started again in a different place. Nobody except our commanders knew what was happening.

On an afternoon in late May, thirty of our company, of which I made one, marched to a rallying point on Scarigg, where we were joined by swords and pikes and a squadron of cavalry, a hundred strong in all. None of us knew what business was in hand, but we had the feeling that battle was imminent, and that we were to be involved.

I remember how we sat together round the fires, talking, drinking, laughing—every man, I swear, with a tight feeling in his belly. We made a meal; then suddenly our captain called on us to stand. As we obeyed there came down a narrow track towards us a tiny cloaked figure on a great grey horse, two yellow hounds loping behind. Even when he drew near few of us recognised him. But when he rode right in amongst us, and signalled us to gather close, we knew him for the Falcon.

We gave him a cheer which he did not deign to acknowledge as he sat looking down at us, all crooked in his saddle, with that fearful crooked smile on his lips. Then he held up his hand, and told us that the enemy were deploying for battle, that the opening skirmishes would take place on the morrow, and that our little force was to be in the van with a very special task to perform. We must confront the enemy, we must fight and so cunningly yield ground that we drew him on and on into the depths of Longdale; and when we had lured all his army there beyond possibility of escape, our own main army would sweep down from the heights, and there would be a mighty killing. The task was formidable and we must not fail; everything depended on trapping the enemy in Longdale. And we would not fail, said he, for although our number was small and the enemy were many, yet one Lakelander was worth a dozen Flemings or fifty Frenchmen; and because of this, we were the greater army.

When he had finished, he sat looking down into our faces, his eyes resting on each man in turn; and we had the feeling that he had taken us one by one to his heart, and that he would never forget us. I was the last man he studied in this way, and as he looked at me I saw, or thought I saw, a light of kindness kindle in his eyes.

"Why, there's our shepherd boy," said he. And when two or three fellows laughed mockingly, he did not mind them, but lifted his hand in salute to me, and said simply: "The best of shepherd boys, the best of bowmen."

And he turned and rode away from us in the mellow evening light.

His words are incised in my heart. With pride I shall remember them till my day of dying.

It was still deep night when we started to march. We climbed the Snab under the soft starlight, and as we began the descent into Belldale, we saw the fires of the enemy camp far beneath us, round and pink like briar buds. It was not yet light when we halted on the lower slopes and built our own fires; not that we needed warmth, for we had marched hard, but it was important that the enemy should be aware of us. Some of our horse went forward and were quickly lost in the gloom. Then we, the archers, spread across the hillside, and took the quivers from our belts, and set them on the ground before us.

So we listened to the enemy movements: horns, horses, voices, far-away sounds from another world. I said my little prayer to God and Gabriel, and watched and waited. With the dawn the clamour strengthened. It came nearer, we heard the clash of arms. Then we saw them, a solid front of cavalry advancing magnificently out of the risen sun, helmets and shields, blades and lances, all flashing as if with fire. Our horsemen had engaged on one wing. Several had fallen, the rest came galloping back.

The enemy came on in a splendid line of horse, not fast but at an easy walk, with the infantry in support. As I watched, I wondered what their thoughts might be, whether they took us for a raggle-taggle peasant mob who would run rather than fight, whether they had ever had a taste of the long bow. I had nocked an arrow on my bowstring and my fingers ached to loose it. I watched the riders in their disciplined approach, each man holding his shield lengthwise in the at-ease position at his left side, as if he feared to sully it, and I wondered at the splendour and the madness of it all. And I thought, they might just as well advance upon us naked, for their hauberks of shining mail would never withstand the arrows of our long bows.

Suddenly our horn sounded. We aimed and loosed.

One, two, three. The line of horses wavered. One, two, three; and then again, one, two, three. It was as if a great and bloody wind had swept through them. The entire disciplined line had gone; it was all fragments, noise, confusion. Men and horses quivered in death. Riderless horses kicked and wheeled in frenzy, horseless riders staggered drunkenly, screaming pain, blossoming blood. We gave them another volley to let them know our quality. Then their infantry came through.

They came running through, crouched under their shields, swerving skilfully this way and that, light as dancers. They made difficult tragets, and for every man we dropped a dozen came on. There was no halting them, it was as if a flood gate had opened. Our horn sounded, and our swordsmen advanced through our lines to cover the retreat. Poor fellows, theirs was a hard duty, for this was a fight we were never meant to win.

We fell back in good order, pausing now and again to loose fresh volleys and so give our swordsmen and our maimed a chance to catch up with us. The fellside is very steep, especially towards the Snab, and though for us it was fairly easy, for the enemy it made fierce, hard going. It was our game to lure them on, and they pursued us slowly and painfully, yet with good courage.

When I looked from the heights of the Snab, all the wide hillside had the appearance of a restless sea, heaving with the bobbing heads of climbing men. Volley after volley we gave them there, and their losses were great, for every arrow claimed its victim. But our losses, too, were grievous, especially amongst the swords and pikes, and when we halted with our backs to Longdale, we had lost nearly half our men.

At that point we made great resistance, as if we must defend at all costs the secret route to Falconsdale. The real route, hidden beneath turf and shrubs, lay a little to our right, and was quite undefended; and we had no means of knowing if our ruse had deceived the enemy captains. Their swords and axes came at us fiercely and in great numbers, but with the help of reinforcements which came up from the dale behind us, we held them fast for several minutes.

My quiver now was empty. I threw down my bow, the best bow in England, and took my sword. It was cut and thrust and give a pace, and cut and thrust again, and the air was thick with cries and the stench of heaving, sweating, bleeding men. The horn sounded and we dropped back fast. Still it sounded and we ran. And the great enemy army poured through the wooded entrance of Longdale behind us, flashing their swords and lances and screaming victory.

And so the trick was done.

Half way down the dale, where it begins to narrow gradually, we stopped again, and the enemy crowded thick upon us, so that it seemed that with every swing of your blade you clove a man's neck or arm or shoulder, and his blood gushed hot in your face and you tasted it on your lips.

Again the horn sounded, again the fast retreat, the craven flight drawing the enemy on and on behind you, until at the western limit of the dale you were confronted with the height of Hagfell; and you turned with a despairing gladness in you because there could be no more running away, you would fight on to the end, you would live or you would die like a true man.

You cut and slashed, you parried, you fell back a pace. A great burden of weariness was with you, your arms sagged, your legs trembled, you could see nothing but a blur of faces all about you. And you thought, They must all be in the trap now, why don't our horns sound, why don't our men strike?

Then it came, the bleat of a horn from the heights. And another, and another. A dozen horns were sounding. And a rain of great stones came down, a deluge of arrows. Then our men, fresh and impatient for the battle, came leaping down from the secret places, leaping from crag to crag, screaming death, their blades flashing.

The enemy surged forward under the pressure of their comrades in the rear. But there was no way out for them. The grey wall of Hagfell faced them. The path of retreat was blocked. They surged forward in panic. In panic they surged back. Some fought wildly with one another, some attempted to climb the steeps of Hagfell. Our men swept down on them in wave after wave.

There never had been such a killing.

I rested that night where we had fought, amongst the uncounted dead. At some time in the night, I know not when, women came there seeking their dead; and their wailing, mixed with the groans of the wounded and the dying, roused me, and I slept no more. Presently I saw Tom and Patrice standing in a glow of firelight, talking with men who had gathered there. The men shook their heads and one pointed down the dale, as if they might find there what they were seeking.

I shouted and sat up quickly. It was like the ending of a terrible dream. The tears stood in Patrice's eyes, but as she knelt to me a look of joy suffused her face; and old Tom stood looking down with his hands clasped and his lips sucked in tight. None of us spoke, and suddenly my soul rose naked and defenceless in me, and I started to cry. I could not help myself. I cried shamelessly, like a weak and silly girl.

Yet, strangely, I think I was happy. Perhaps that is the truth of it: I cried for happiness that yesterday was yesterday and done with, and today was now, and my friends had found me.

Farewell 21

WE BUILT many fires in Longdale and made many pyres for the enemy dead. Our own dead comrades, numbering five hundred and twenty, we carried up into the fells and buried under mounds, some at Barton Howe, some at Tottle Howe, high and desolate places where the warm west winds blow unceasingly.

To our dismay, neither Ralf nor William Meschin was amongst the dead. How those two French weasels escaped the trap which had caught so many of their hirelings nobody can say; but so it was. As it happens it may not matter overmuch, for the defeat of their army (an army paid for by the Royal Treasury) was so total, so overwhelming, that both leaders are said to be quite discredited with the King and their fellow barons, too. And as a direct result of our victory, we can now move freely along the whole of the western coast from Providence to Ravenglass, and our ships trade without hindrance with Ireland, Man, and Wales.

Within a month of the battle, the Falcon summoned me and offered me an honoured post in his household. I begged to be excused, though I told him I was his sworn man and would serve him faithfully when the need arose. He took my hand with the kindness he now always showed to me.

"In my lifetime the need will not arise—nor perhaps in yours, Alan. It depends not upon Ralf Meschin, who has become a jest, but upon the King of England—and who can read that riddle of a man? You have gifts, Alan—letters, languages, a marksman with the bow, yes, these are great gifts. But I make no claim on you, you have served us well. Now you may go back to old Tom and Wilfrid's daughter, who are busy with the shearing, for there I know your heart lies."

And so I joined them in Cordale, and helped with the shearing; and when that long task was done, we went up to Birk Crags, driving the shorn flocks before us. And as of old, the land laid its spell upon me: the glory of another fine summer, the colours and the hard autumn rains, the wildness and whiteness of a winter, it was all so dear and close to me, as if time had never passed.

But often now I recall Earl Bueth's words, and I wonder that he of all men could speak of Henry of England with that sort of guarded tolerance—a "riddle of a man." I ask myself, What riddle there can be about a son of William the Bastard and a brother of the Red King? Is he not of the brood that has wreaked endless misery and suffering upon the English? Is he not likewise to be hated and despised?

Some men, good Englishmen, too, think otherwise. I have talked with these men in the long winter nights by crackling firesides, I have argued endlessly with them. And although I do not pretend to share their notions, I must strive to report truthfully what they say—for who but God and King Henry can say who is right and who is wrong?

And true, I do not know this King Henry, I have never spoken with him. I saw him but once or twice in Winchester, when he was reckoned a prince of very small account.

By general consent he is hard, ruthless, scholarly (they nickname him Beauclerk), and of a subtle, scheming turn of mind. Some think he plotted the murder of the Red King, and certainly the keys of the Royal Treasury were in his hands within a few hours of the death of Rufus. Others say yes, but all kings are schemers, and a man is not a villain merely because he schemes. And they say that Henry dislikes and distrusts the Norman barons whom the Bastard, his own father, thrust on the English as their overlords, and in proof of Henry's intentions they point to the Charter which he has but lately drawn up.

It is a curious thing, this Charter. By its terms, some clear, some vague, Henry promises to bring order to the land and to restore to the Church those incomes which Rufus plundered from it. The barons are excused certain feudal duties on payment of good monies to the King; the English law of Edward is to be restored; Curfew and the tax called Danegeld are to be abolished; the barons are commanded to accord justice to their under-tenants and to cease in all unfair demands upon them.

These are fair words for Englishmen. Whether deeds will justify the words only time will show. But the greatness of Henry and the real proof of his intentions (they say) is shown in his marriage. The story of the marriage is strange indeed and has the flavour of a fable, but I believe it is true, as I record it, in all particulars.

Thus it goes. Until recently there walked the cloisters of the Abbey of Romsey, which is close to Winchester, a young nun called Matilda the Good. Her baptised name is Eadgyth; she is a princess of Scotland, and a niece of Edgar Atheling; the blood of Alfred the Great and many another noble Englishman runs in her veins. The name of Matilda was probably bestowed on her by the forthright Abbess of Romsey, her own aunt Christina, who has a tart tongue and a pair of fists which she does not hesitate to use in furtherance of the Will of God.

When King Henry declared his intention of marrying Matilda, he was warned by the Abbess that Matilda had taken vows and veil, and was thereby given to God and denied to mortal men, including England's King. Mindful of the Holy Laws, Henry asked Archbishop Anselm to inquire well into the matter and the Lady Matilda was summoned to the Archbishop's Court. This question then was put to her:

"Why did you choose the veil, Matilda?"

"As God is my judge," she answered, sobbing, "I chose nothing. But this veil was forced on me by the hard words and hard slappings of my aunt. Out of her presence I have many times torn the veil from my head and stamped on it."

She was granted dispensation and the King immediately married her, to the indignation of the barons who mock her secretly, though many common people rejoice, thinking that since English and French are now united under the Crown, so the two nations will soon blend into one.

Well, as I say, I find it hard to believe; my hatred of the French cuts deep. Yet with all my heart I hope it is so, for I have had my sickening fill of war and killing. Those who love battles can have them, I am no great captain. I am most content as I am; and though sometimes seeking a day of liberty to hunt a deer or a wild boar with my bow, I will always return to mind my sheep, here under the wind-blown skies of the fairest land on earth.

But Patrice has other plans in mind.

I am writing these last words of my book where I started it, in the heather high above Falconsdale. There stamps old Tom across the slope, a puppy trailing his heels, as he rounds up a dozen sheep that have climbed on to the Crags. Patrice sits beside me. She is plumper, rounder than she was a year and a half ago, but no taller, thanks be. She is acquiring a pretty woman's shape and in her own dark way she is rather beautiful. One day I will tell her so; but not yet, it will give her vain ideas. Her character has not altered: she is impetuous, petulant, tender, brave. Also she has developed a sort of clumsy guile, a roundabout way of making me aware of what she feels.

Her dark eyes are on me now, and I can guess pretty well what is passing in her mind. After a long silence, she says:

"Earl Bueth is an old man."

"Yes."

"He can't live for ever."

"No."

"What will happen when he dies?"

"We will choose another Falcon, another Leader."

"Perhaps they will make you Leader."

"I don't want to be Leader."

"But they might *make* you. You were good in the battle, everyone says so. They might make you Leader, they might call you lord, like Earl Bueth. If you were a lord, that would make me a noble lady, wouldn't it?"

"No."

"Yes, it would! If you were King I should be Queen, shouldn't I?"

"Only if I married you."

I keep my face very straight as I say it. She stares at me. Her mouth trembles a little. She cries:

"Who else is going to marry you?"

"Oh, there are a lot of fine ladies."

"What ladies?"

"Why, in Winchester I saw . . ."

"You don't know any fine ladies in Winchester!" she screams. "And if you do, you shan't marry any one but me! You wretch, do you hear? You're going to marry *me!*"

She stands over me, her eyes flashing and her fists clenched, ready to pound me into submission. I won't submit just yet, but one of these days she will have her way with me, I know.

I love her, and I am glad of it.